HOW NOT TO GET SHOT

Also by D. L. Hughley

BLACK MAN, WHITE HOUSE

HOW NOT TO GET SHOT

And Other Advice from White People

D.L. HUGHLEY

AND DOUG MOE

WILLIAM MORROW
An Imprint of HarperCollins*Publishers*

Flowchart on p. 95 by Springer Cartographics, LLC

Courtesy of Shutterstock: "Wise Words" icon (p. 11, 173): Dolimac; "DLialogue" icon (pp. 11, 145, 180, 224): LINE ICONS; "Tip" icon (p. 12): Vladvm; "Remember" icon (p. 12, 124, 191): Johnny Sajem; "Anecdote" icon (pp. 13, 14, 133, 182, 217): Sabelskaya; "Did You Know?" icon (p. 13): Volhah; "Let's Meet!" icon (pp. 13, 110, 158): Quarta; "Stuff White People Say" icon (pp. 14, 47, 57, 87, 173): Rudie Strummer; pp. 47, 57, 196: pathdoc; p. 54: KennyK.com; p. 65: Monkey Business Images; p. 66, top: Photographee.eu; p. 66, bottom, p. 67: michaeljung; p. 78: studiostoks; p. 79: Africa Studio; p. 87: Vladimir Gjorgiev; p. 100: Featureflash Photo Agency; p. 102: sbukley; p. 104: Noel Powell; p. 107, top: Joshua Rainey Photography; p. 107, bottom: Rawpixel.com; p. 108: Lucky Business; p. 121, left: Gino Santa Maria; p. 121, right: stockyimages; p. 132: Prokopeva Irina; p. 173: wavebreakmedia; p. 197, top: Voltgroup; p. 197, bottom: Christos Georghiou; p. 198: Blend Images; p. 209: Charles Haire; pp. 210, 211: BestPix.

Other credits: p. 69, 70, 129, bottom: Gage Skidmore; p. 110: U.S. Department of Justice; p. 117: Government of Japan; p. 127: official White House photo by D. Myles Cullen; p. 128, top: United States Department of the Treasury; p. 128, bottom: Frantz Jantzen; p. 129, top: official White House photo by Shealah Craighead; p. 158: Karppinen.

HarperCollins books may be purchased for educational, business, or sales promotional use. For information, please email the Special Markets Department at SPsales@harpercollins.com.

FIRST EDITION

DESIGNED BY WILLIAM RUOTO

Library of Congress Cataloging-in-Publication Data has been applied for.

ISBN 978-0-06-269854-4

18 19 20 21 22   LSC   10 9 8 7 6 5 4 3 2 1

This book is dedicated to my son, Kyle.

Contents

HOW NOT TO GET SHOT

INTRODUCTION

Tamir Rice
Michael Brown
Philando Castile

And on it goes.

In America, a black dude is three times more likely to be killed in encounters with police than a white guy. If you're black, you already know why #thisbookmatters.

This might be the most important book you buy this year, you cheap mofo. After all, if you get shot, how the heck are you gonna read more books? You're dead.

This stuff has been going on so long, I don't know if a book can help, but why not try?

That's why I present to you *How Not to Get Shot: And Other Advice from White People,* a how-to guide for black people, full of advice from white people, translated by me, a black guy. Got it? Oh, and pass the book along to white people, too.

And if you're Asian or Latino, let me be the first black man to give you some advice: buy this book now because once we're gone you'll be next.

But, D.L., is this a joke?

I'm a comedian, but I'm serious. You know how you try to baby-proof your home by putting little things over the outlets? Well, this book is like that: I'm gonna try to police-shoot-proof black people as much as we can. Will it work? Who knows? I mean, sometimes a kid still sticks his fork in a plug and gets zapped—but it's still worth a try, right?

I started thinking about this a little bit ago, when I went on Megyn Kelly's Fox News show to get lectured about the killing of Philando Castile, getting told yet again that if a black man had just followed police orders he wouldn't have ended up shot dead. This was before America decided Kelly wasn't racist anymore and let her move from Fox News Channel to NBC. That time it was Philando Castile, but it could have been Michael Brown, Tamir Rice, or Keith Scott. Or Alton Sterling. Or Walter Scott. Or Stephon Clark.

I had Megyn Kelly telling me that "we don't know if Philando threatened a police officer with his gun," presuming yet again the innocence of the police over the innocence of the victim. Of course, now we do know what happened—a police officer shot a man for no reason. Big surprise. And then they stacked a jury with pro-police white guys and he got off, of course.

When these incidents happen, black people hear this over and over: "Who knows what happened?" And then we get the inevitable advice on how these victims should have acted differently:

- "Comply with police orders."
- "Don't resist arrest."
- "Don't break the law and you won't get shot."

White people are always giving out "helpful" advice. These mofos have been doling out tips to black people ever since "I suggest you pick the cotton if you don't like gettin' whipped." It seemed crazy to me that we keep hearing this stuff over and over.

But then I had a moment of clarity: What if they were right? What if Megyn Kelly was actually onto something?

See, for a little while there, it seemed like white people were on their way out, what with a black president and everything. But now we know that Barack was just the intermission and it's back to the real show. It's "Welcome back, niggas. The show must go on."

Look, we're in a different place now. If Trump can get elected after everything we know about him, maybe white people know what they're talking about, right? This is a guy who was heard on tape saying he likes to grab women's pussies; made stupid red hats a fashion item after spreading racist lies that Barack Obama wasn't born in America; buddied up with Vladimir Putin . . . but he's still our president. We ain't in Kenya anymore! Let's face it: the White Man is back.

How did this happen? I blame Nat Turner. In 1831, that

dude had his slave rebellion, scared white people, and basi-cally ruined it for all black people. That was one of the first times that a black dude did something, hundreds of miles away, that f-ed stuff up for *everybody*. Some black dude's like, "Mofo, I'm just trying to get work, I ain't rising up!" and then he got hung.

Ask any old black southerner: they all know the story of the slave uprising, because it was incredible: even when black people were slaves, white people were afraid. And that fear was about losing control of black people. Before "black-on-black crime," before we asked to vote, before #BlackLivesMatter, we were be-ing shot and hung by the police. Police are basically doing now what they've always done, which is to keep niggers in their place. Whether it was removing us from a lunch counter or telling us to get back across the line or hanging us for made-up reasons, they have always been the agent of bringing black people to heel.

So unarmed black people getting killed isn't new, it's retro. Today, it's unarmed black people getting killed in high-def and on camera phones. The technology is new, but the story is old. Used to be, you had to wait for some mofo to make a drawing—now we got the killing on Facebook Live or on a body cam, if we're lucky. Have you ever noticed how when something happens that people don't want you to know about, their body cam goes off?

But when they do have body-cam footage, that oughta settle it, right? Video should be proof, but somehow it isn't. After all, what good is a grand jury looking at a body cam video if they don't have bias-proof glasses?

So that's the way I've always seen things. But Megyn Kelly woke me up. See, we've been trying to insist on equal rights, having a voice, police reform—but we forgot that white people are the arbiters of knowing everything. Maybe we should listen to the wisdom they're offering us?

And after all, not getting shot by the police has always been a problem for black people; even when we had a black president! Now that we have a new set of overlords, with President Trump at the helm, wouldn't it be nice to get a little advice on how not to get shot? And maybe even how to dress and listen to music?

So no black person wants to hear another bit of advice from a white person, even if they aren't as full of crap as Megyn Kelly or Donald Trump. They're so tired of it all. I get it. But maybe I, D. L. Hughley, can help bridge this divide. Perhaps I can take on the mantle of this burden. Maybe I can police-shoot-proof a few black people by listening to the arbiters of what's right and wrong.

That's why I've decided to compile the best pieces of advice together in one book: *How Not to Get Shot: And Other Advice from White People*, the etiquette guide that black people didn't know they needed until White America doubled down on White Power.

HOW TO USE THIS BOOK

NOTE: If you're in immediate danger of being shot by the police, put down this book and keep your hands where the police can see them. You're not Luke Cage and this book isn't made of titanium and it won't make you bullet-proof. Cops don't usually shoot people holding books, but you never know what might "look like a gun."

Okay, so you are tired of getting advice from white people about what to do and how to act. It feels like you can't turn on the TV or read a newspaper without some white guy telling you how to live your life and how to be. I know.

But what if I told you that following the advice of white people could make you happier, healthier, and a little less threatening to white people? Wouldn't you like to know why white people are the way they are? Wouldn't it be good to know why they're being such dicks all the time?

No? Okay, well, wouldn't you at least like to make fun of them for a bit? Okay then, great! Keep reading.

HOW TO USE THIS BOOK

You know how to use books, so I don't want to overexplain it.

The book is divided into five sections:

1. How to Not Get Shot by the Police

2. How to Look

3. How to Act

4. Understanding White People

5. Tidbits of Advice for White People from Black People

In each section, I'll present a quote from the most prominent purveyors of white culture to get the best advice possible; everything from Bill O'Reilly's guidance on how to name your kids to Mark Fuhrman's instructions on speaking politely. Then I'll translate this advice into practical tips to improve your black experience by making it whiter. Each section will feature specific bits of helpful advice such as "How to be nice and quiet" and "How to wear your hair" along with charts and graphics to keep you from getting too bored.

WHITE PEOPLE ADVICE THROUGH THE AGES: A HISTORY

White people have been giving advice for as long as anyone can remember there being white people. Before that it was probably hairy people receiving advice on how not to get speared by less hairy people. They probably had an #AllNeanderthalsMatter crowd back then, too. That's actually not a joke: scientists now believe that early European humans were responsible for killing off their (bigger-brained) Neanderthal cousins forty thousand years ago. This shit is in white people's DNA! If Neanderthals had had this book, maybe they'd be around today.

But here we are in the twenty-first century. We find ourselves at a unique point in history where black people shouldn't *have* to listen to white people, and yet white people still have lots of advice to give. Let's look at white people advice through the ages:

- **1619–1865:** SLAVERY: Advice is a bit more . . . mandatory.
- **1896–1965:** JIM CROW—A lot of helpful white people advice starts with "boy," as in "Boy, you better not look at me that way," not "Boy, I'd like to buy some black people ice cream." Other white people advice: where

to sit, what water fountain to drink from, what part of the country to flee.

- **1970s:** "Why can't you be more like *Roots*?"
- **1980s:** Why can't you be more like that nice boy Michael Jackson?
- **1990s:** If Rodney King had just complied with police orders . . .
- **2000s:** White people discover another bunch of scary colored people: Muslims. The heat is off.
- **OBAMA ERA:** Lalalalala, I don't have to listen to you anymore. Fuck you, white people!
- **TRUMP ERA:** Oh shit, my bad. What was that, white people?

ICONS USED IN THIS BOOK

Throughout this book you'll find eight or so sidebars that will help make the process of learning even easier. I might add more later. I haven't decided. Don't pressure me. It's the beginning of the book:

"WISE WORDS"

These special boxes include quotes from all sorts of people that will guide and inspire you.

"DLIALOGUE"

Sometimes I just gotta say something in my own words. And that's when I'll give you a DLialogue. I know that's a fucked-up-looking term, but it's my book, so I'll do what I want. When you write your own book, you can call it what the fuck you want!

"TIP"

Just like the tips white tourists leave when they visit Harlem, these tips are all a bit patronizing.

"REMEMBER"

"Remember" is just a tip by another name, but I gotta fill this book somehow.

"ANECDOTE"

Not to be confused with "remember," an "anecdote" is a
short personal story that I'm remembering.

"DID YOU KNOW?"

These are short bits of statistics or other real bits of information.

"LET'S MEET!"

Enjoy these short profiles of notable white people and
their inspiring life stories.

"STUFF WHITE PEOPLE SAY"

Here we'll listen to what some white people say, even if we don't want to.

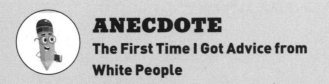

ANECDOTE
The First Time I Got Advice from White People

My earliest memory of receiving advice from white people was from teachers commenting on my school work. They wanted to talk about how I wasn't applying myself—not that I just didn't get it. I don't know if I wasn't trying or if I, in fact, just couldn't. Nobody knew I had a learning disability that they hadn't diagnosed. They thought it was just that I didn't apply myself. I wasn't trying. Not much has changed for black kids in school.

But that's the first time I remember getting advice from white people. They seemed to have all the answers. They always knew what to do.

You have to understand, I grew up on 135th and Avalon in South Central Los Angeles, so the only white people in my neighborhood were the policemen, the teachers, and the insurance men. Those were the only whites around. The insurance men were there because, in my neighborhood, all deaths were sad, but not all deaths were shocking. So some mothers and fathers saved a college fund for their kid, and some just bought extra insurance. "Because if this motherfucker's gonna get killed in the streets, I'm gonna get me a new car."

So as a kid, the only white folks I knew seemed to have all the answers: they were in charge of teaching, security, and making sure people got a payout if the whole thing went wrong.

PART I

HOW TO NOT GET SHOT BY THE POLICE

In this part, we're gonna get right into it and make sure you know how to not get shot by the police. First of all, we're going to figure out the *right* way to talk to the police so they feel more empowered to not shoot you. Then we'll take a look at how to put cops at ease, since being a cop can be very scary, especially when you're dealing with very scary black people. And if you do get shot, let's not rush to judgment. Sure, being shot can be upsetting but we don't want to paint all cops with the same brush. After all, they've been through a traumatic experience.

Are you ready to not get shot? Let's go!

1

COMPLY WITH POLICE ORDERS

"Here is the bottom line: if you don't want to get shot, tased, pepper-sprayed, struck with a baton, or thrown to the ground, just do what I tell you."

—Sunil Dutta, LAPD officer and adjunct instructor of homeland security at Colorado Technical University

"Comply with police orders!"

That's the first thing you'll hear from white people: if you don't want to get shot, just comply. If a black person gets shot by the police, white people ask: "Why didn't they just do what the officer said?" White people can't understand it: it seems so simple.

Is it that simple? I wish it was. Let's make sure you're complying the *right* way.

COMPLY WITH THE *SPIRIT* OF THE ORDER

Just do what the cop says. But also make sure you are complying with the *spirit* of the request. A police officer wants you to comply with both their command and the way they want it done.

Let's take Philando Castile. Philando Castile was shot when he reached for his wallet. Officer Jeronimo Yanez asked him for his license and registration and then he got shot. Why? Because he didn't comply with the *spirit of the request.*

Put yourself in Officer Yanez's shoes: He pulls over a random black guy because he's seeking a robbery suspect. Officer Yanez spotted Philando's "wide-set nose" that "matched the description" of a robbery suspect. Did the robbery suspect also have a girlfriend and a child in his car? Well, robberies are weird—you never know if that baby in the back is a tiny gangster dressed up as a baby or something.

Officer Yanez smelled marijuana. What kind of a monster smokes marijuana in front of their kid? Bear in mind this is not Colorado, where marijuana is legal. Or California. Or Alaska, Maine, Massachusetts, Nevada, Oregon, and Washington. In Minnesota, weed is still a very dangerous drug.

So he's obviously scared. He's got a dangerous robbery suspect, high on marijuana with his robber girlfriend and robber baby. He asks for Philando's license and registration. Did Philando comply? Yes and no.

He did comply by reaching for his wallet. But then Philando tells the officer that he has a gun. We know that Philando mentioned this so that the officer would be aware of it and not be scared. But it does the opposite. It scares him. He freaks out. Officer Yanez doesn't know why this dangerous criminal is announcing he has a gun. And even though Philando is reaching for his license as he was asked to do, Officer Yanez assumes he's reaching for his gun and shoots him.

So, no, he didn't comply. He complied with the order, but not the *spirit of the order*. The spirit of the order was to get his license while not being so *dangerous*. What would have made Philando less dangerous? Maybe Philando shouldn't have had a gun at all. Philando assumed that he was allowed to have a gun, but he didn't see that he couldn't comply with the spirit of the orders while exercising his Second Amendment rights. Or maybe if he had it, he shouldn't have told the police and just waited to be thrown to the ground when they discovered it and hope to not be shot then. Or maybe he should have had it sitting out on his dashboard so it would be clear that when he reached for his wallet, he wasn't reaching for his gun.

Maybe none of that would have helped. After all, according to a report in the *Washington Post*, blacks are the most likely to be shot by police. *The most likely*. And that's irrespective of socioeconomic background. So it's not just poor black people at risk. It's rich black folks, too. In other words, rich black people still get shot at a disproportionately high rate. So you can't get away from the mitigating factor being race. It's nice to be rich, but you can't buy your way out of being black.

Let's just face it, black people . . . We're a very target-y-looking group. We look shootable. By being black, you're not complying with the *spirit of the order*, which is "get in your place, nigga."

COMPLY WITH POLICE ORDERS *FAST*

Be sure to comply with police orders quickly—an officer might decide that you are moving too slow and that shooting you is a better option. Once an officer asks you to do something, there's a timer ticking. You don't have forever to comply.

A lot of times you have almost no time at all. The cops roll up and start firing almost as soon as they arrive, like with Tamir Rice or John Crawford.

COMPLY WITH POLICE ORDERS *SLOWLY*

But then again, some people get shot for moving *too* fast. In South Carolina, in 2014, Levar Jones was asked for his license and he quickly went to get it from his truck. He moved so quick that the state trooper shot him for "lunging" into his vehicle. Jones said, "Why did you shoot me?" The cop said, "Well, you dove headfirst back into your car."

So that argues for moving slowly. *No lunging.* No diving

headfirst. But don't move too slowly or it might seem like you're being menacing (see above).

WHAT IF I DON'T UNDERSTAND HOW TO COMPLY?

The fastest way to get shot by police in America is by being mentally or emotionally unstable. According to a report by the Ruderman Family Foundation, almost half of the people shot by police have some kind of disability. They are mentally or physically or emotionally disabled. And the police are most often the first responders to mental health situations. So even if they are issuing commands, there needs to be training so police don't just shoot people for "noncompliance."

How is a mentally ill person supposed to comply with police orders? In multiple instances, when police were informed that a person was mentally ill, they still shot that person instead of using less deadly force. Schizophrenics, people off their meds, and people with brain injuries are all treated as if they can comply. Like Laquan McDonald, who was shot by police even though he was surrounded by police who were in no danger. Meanwhile, he suffered from PTSD and other mental health disorders. Or take Keith Scott, whose wife took video of the police confronting her husband. On the video, she's trying to get the police to understand that he had a traumatic brain injury, that he was disabled. But even though he was complying with their orders to back up, he may not have fully understood what was being asked of him. Rather than treat the situation with patience and care, the officers shot him.

So if you don't understand how to comply because of a disability, you'd better hope that you're not not understanding how to comply in one of the thirty-four states that don't mandate de-escalation training. If you're lucky, you'll be in Dallas, where excessive force complaints dropped by 18 percent the year after they put the training into effect. That's maybe the only reason you'd be lucky to be in Dallas.

WHAT IF I'M A KID?

When I was a kid, I learned compliance from my mom. My mother would always tell me the rules before we left the house to go get groceries: "Don't look at shit, don't touch shit, you ain't getting shit." And sometimes I even listened to her.

But with the police, being a kid does not exempt you from complying. If you're Tamir Rice, playing with a toy gun in the park, your compliance is requested even if you're doing nothing wrong.

It's hard to get kids to follow directions in normal circumstances. But if the police are giving orders to a kid, the kid better pay a lot more attention to the police than I did to my mama. With the police, a child has to act more responsibly than a trained professional. Especially if the trained professional isn't really trained or professional. The cop who shot and killed Tamir had resigned from his previous job in the Independence Police Department because he was about to be fired. Why? Because he couldn't follow "basic functions as instructed," according to his old boss, the deputy police chief. That didn't stop Cleveland from hiring him, though.

This officer shot Tamir almost immediately. Maybe he yelled something from within the car, or perhaps not. It depends on whether you believe the officer's video statement he gave to police right after the shooting or whether you believe his written testimony later. Or maybe you trust the surveillance video that showed him practically leap out of the car and start shooting. One of those three is bound to be right.

Tamir is supposed to comply with police orders within two seconds of a police car screeching to a halt in front of him. See, when a police officer can't comply, he gets hired. When a kid can't comply, he gets shot. Being a kid is tough.

WHAT IF I DON'T HAVE TIME TO COMPLY?

In Tamir's case, it's hard to see how he could have complied with police orders even if he had heard any. Sometimes the police just roll up and start firing. Take John Crawford in Dayton, Ohio: He was in a Walmart, carrying around a BB gun that he intended to buy, talking on his phone. The cops came in and shot him before he was able to do anything.

Sometimes you don't have time to comply, so you have to pre-comply. You have to think about what kind of threat you would be if you became one. Pre-complying means knowing that you aren't allowed to hold a BB gun in a Walmart. Toy guns are a big pre-compliance no-no.

It's too bad you don't see more black magicians. Because to avoid being shot, you gotta be a mind reader. Pre-comply at all times, if possible. Pre-compliance means anticipating compliance and being available to comply at any moment.

Compliance Request	How to Be Pre-Compliant
"Drop the gun"	Don't have a gun, toy gun, wallet, dark thing
"Hands in the air"	Have your hands free, not in your pockets; not holding something
"Don't move"	Minimize movement. If already moving, be able to stop quickly; don't be fast
"Get on the ground"	Stay close to the ground; don't be tall; wear stuff you could get dirty

So if John Crawford had pre-complied, he wouldn't have been holding a toy gun that he was going to buy while casually talking to his girlfriend on the phone in an open-carry state. If John Crawford had pre-complied he might still be alive today.

WHAT IF I AM WHITE?

If you are white, comply at your leisure. In Kalamazoo, Michigan, an old white dude with a rifle was standing around yelling at people and cars in front of a Dairy Queen. Multiple 911 calls later, a bunch of cops rolled up and he mouthed off to them and didn't comply with their orders. He wouldn't put his weapon down, so of course they fucking shot the dude.

Oh wait, did I say that the cops shot the dude? I meant they *didn't* shoot the dude. You know, a white guy with a real rifle shouting about revolution can tell a cop that he's "acting like a prick" and not get dropped. He wasn't even charged because Michigan is an open-carry state. "But, DL, I thought you said that John Crawford was in an open-carry state, and he got shot. How come this old white dude didn't get shot?" It's simple: because a nigga with a *play* gun is more dangerous than a raging white dude with a *real* gun.

So if you're white, take your time complying, open-carry all you want. Old white guys are still in charge! If you're black, stay pre-compliant so you won't look target-y.

SUMMARY

Like white people say: it's easy to not get shot if you just comply with police orders. So whatever you do, obey. Comply with orders even if they contradict each other or are shouted at you suddenly from behind a drawn gun. Comply with them if they are unreasonable, demeaning, or weird. In fact, it would be best to be clairvoyant so you can comply with orders *before* the cop has even thought of what he wants you to do. Complying is the only way to ensure that you're not as target-y.

- If you're not sure how to comply, be sure to comply with what you think the cop *meant*.
- Comply quickly, but not too quickly.
- Comply slowly, but not too slowly.
- Play guns are for white people.

Complying is simple when you follow these simple rules!

2

DON'T TALK BACK

"From the time that he pulled that car over, he was very personable, he was calm, he was polite. He called her 'ma'am' several times. And he could sense that she was irritated and he asked her. She was loaded for bear from the time that she pulled over. I expect, in those situations, an officer to make a reasonable attempt to de-escalate a situation, but not to put him or her in harm's way while doing it. So once that fails, I expect an officer to go into arrest mode. And that's what he did. Once you go into arrest mode, you get to move up on the force continuum—it's no longer verbal commands. You can use intermediate weapons—he chose a taser."

—Sheriff David Clarke

"It's just a good policy: even if you know the cop is
in the wrong, comply and complain later."
—Megyn Kelly, *The Kelly Files*, July 23, 2016

There are many reasons people might get shot by the police
(being black, being in the wrong place at the wrong time, etc.)
and you can't control all of them. But you can control how you
talk to the police.

You may not be looking forward to talking to the police.
And guess what? They may not be looking forward to talking
to you, either! What should you say? How can you relate to
them and get out of the conversation? You have so little in
common: they're a person with a gun in an organization with
a history of racial bias and white supremacy and you're a black
person. There's a word for that: "awkward!"

Here we have Megyn Kelly and Sheriff David Clarke
talking about the stopping of Sandra Bland, which eventually ended in her being arrested (and her alleged suicide in
jail). This traffic stop is a case study in how white people view
speaking with the police. And we're lucky enough to have one
of the most prominent Trump-era white journalists, Megyn
Kelly, recently elevated from Fox News to NBC, and her guest
Sheriff David Clarke, a strict law-and-order favorite black person that Trump tried to appoint to the Department of Homeland Security before everyone freaked out.

Here, our white expert and her lackey are contrasting the police officer's politeness with Sandra Bland's "irritation." As described by Sheriff Clarke, the police officer acts just the way you'd want a police officer to act: "personable," "calm," and "polite." He "called her ma'am several times." Very nice. Of course, a little later he was threatening to "light her up," but at least in this part of their conversation, he was a perfect gentleman.

Sandra Bland was smoking a cigarette and seemed "irritated," which is understandable because she probably didn't think she should have been pulled over. But when the officer asked her to put out her cigarette, she asked why she had to. I'm going to assume Sandra did seem irritated. Of course, it's impossible to tell what her demeanor was from the dashboard cam of Officer Encinia's police car, and his testimony is suspect (he was indicted on perjury charges, which were later dismissed).

Can you spot the faux pas in Sandra Bland's approach? In the face of a polite officer, merely pulling over a black woman for an illegal lane change, Sandra Bland was rude. She was "loaded for bear." Never mind that an illegal lane change is a bullshit excuse to pull over someone! Any white person will tell you that being rude is not the right approach! Megyn Kelly says it well: "It's just good policy; even if you know the cop is in the wrong, comply and complain later."

SMALL TALK WITH POLICE

In a way, talking to police is just a little bit of involuntary small talk. It's one of those things that white people excel at: chit-chat. But with, you know, slightly higher stakes.

I couldn't get Miss Manners on the phone, but that's fine. That's why I have the Internet. I did a quick Google search on "How to make small talk" to get some pointers for us. This shit looks as good or better than if I had laid out money for an "expert." Here's eight tips:

1. "Look approachable and friendly"

At a party, you might hope that someone wants to talk to you, so you want to seem friendly and approachable. Here, the cop is approaching you whether or not you seem approachable. It's not exactly the same, but try to be friendly! When you've been hassled by the cops a bunch of times, you might not feel very friendly, but think about what happens to unfriendly black people.

2. "Seem open nonverbally before you start talking"

Not in a way that says "I'm drunk" or "too high to talk." And not in a nonverbal way that makes it seem like you might not speak English, or that might make them think you're a Mexican that should be kicked out of the country. Nonverbal in a "I don't want to waste your time" way. Nonverbal in an

"I'm innocent" way. Don't seem like you don't want to talk. You do! Try to seem relaxed and happy to eventually start talking.

Seeming irritated and "knowing your rights" can come across as not very "open."

3. "Open with a small interaction"

Huh. Well, at a cocktail party, you might say something like "Man, this bar is slammed tonight." But that'd probably be the wrong thing to say to a cop. . . . In a way, rolling down your window is already a small interaction. Yeah. Give yourself credit for this one. Good job!

4. "Introduce yourself"

Showing your license and registration may not be the way you'd like to introduce yourself, but you probably have to. That's usually introduction enough.

5. "Ask open-ended questions"

Okay, I think this isn't really applicable. Not everything from the Internet is going to work.

6. "Ask the person to explain something to you"

Like "Why the fuck am I being pulled over?" Okay, actually skip this one, too.

7. "Don't be afraid to disagree"
Skip this.

8. "Stick to safe topics"
Like ending the conversation as soon as possible.

Okay, that's probably enough free advice from the Web—
you get what you pay for. Next time I'll spring for an expert.

At a party, you might end up getting someone's number.
But if you mess up this bit of small talk with a cop, your number may be up.

BE POLITE

Maybe talking to the police is less fun than chit chat at your
office party. Maybe it's not really small talk. But that doesn't
mean you can't be polite. That's one thing white people definitely like to point out: just be polite to cops!

Of course, there are exceptions to this rule. Remember
when tennis star James Blake got manhandled in New York
during the US Open? He didn't have time to be polite because he was getting his ass thrown to the ground. He was
standing outside his hotel in midtown Manhattan when
a cop ran up out of nowhere and tackled and cuffed him.
As the former fourth-ranked tennis player in the world, he
probably would have been polite! Tennis is a very traditional

sport—it's *steeped* in tradition. When you have to wear white tennis shorts all the time, you tend to be polite. And he probably would have been, had it not been for the fact that he had a cop's boot in his ass.

So there are times when you can't be polite.

DON'T BE SASSY

Talking to police is not the time to demonstrate your wit. For some reason, cops can find sass in the smallest of places. They are expecting some sassy back talk and they do not like it. Talking to cops is a good time to practice your best manners.

Maybe you've been provoked—there have been a couple of times that cops have been caught on camera saying stuff that wasn't very polite. Maybe more than a couple of times. Cops sure like to talk a lot of shit, but when you talk back to them, they act shocked, especially if they hear profanity.

Sassy, meat-headed cops with an attitude—that's what we've come to expect. But that's why you have to be extra sweet. Maybe some of you can throw on a "honey" or a "sugar" instead of a "sir" and pull it off. It's never worked for me.

I've been known to say shit that gets me in trouble. So if you're like me, you need a little help to not let your mouth get you in trouble. If you tend to be the type of person who likes a snappy comeback, allow me to translate some of your witticisms into cop-appropriate responses:

Cop: Do you know why I pulled you over?

Bad response: Yes, I do know because I can read your mind! Let me look into my fucking crystal ball . . . hmmm, it looks like you pulled me over because you don't like black people!

Good response: No, Officer.

Cop: Where are you going in such a hurry?

Bad response: On my way to fuck your mother and then to my drug dealer's house, you racist piece of shit!

Good response: I'm sorry, Officer.

Cop: You were going way over the speed limit.

Bad response: Fuck you!

Good response: I'm mortified and very sorry, sir.

Cop: I'm going to let you off with a warning.

Bad response—Ya know what, they never just let you off with a warning. Fuck it.

SAY "SIR"

Be sure to call the police officer "sir." A carefully placed "sir" can work wonders for a white officer's attitude.

For a white person, there's something about being called "sir" that whisks them away to a more genteel time. I don't know, there's just something about it that makes them feel nostalgic. . . . It puts white people at ease, like sipping an iced tea on a porch in summertime. One can almost hear the old train whistle blowing, bringing the boys back home. It's like watching *Gone with the Wind*—it makes them lament the good old days. Back when America was great and they could fill their lungs with the sweet summer air while the june bugs sang a piece. Back when white people didn't suffer from "white privilege" or be taken to task for acknowledging their primacy in the world. They were giants—allowed to reign and make the world their own by their own benevolence.

And hearing "sir" means that you get it. You *get it.* It means that you've been trained well. And that they're back in charge or that their being in charge is acknowledged, maybe even preferred.

SUMMARY

When you're talking to cops, try not to be rude. Even if the cop is less than a gentleman, you don't want to give him or her any excuse to get mad with you, or worse. Like Sheriff Clarke said, even though you might *think* you're in a conversation, you might *actually* be getting "verbal commands." After that, they can move up the "force continuum." Once you move up the force continuum, talking's over, maybe permanently.

REMEMBER:

- Don't be rude.
- Be approachable and friendly.
- Even if you know the cop is in the wrong, comply and complain later (let's make sure there's a later).
- Talking to cops is just like highly dangerous chitchat, except instead of finding out if it's raining later, you might be finding out that you're dead.

3

DON'T BREAK THE LAW!

The best part of reading white people advice on the Internet is seeing how it's all laid out so simply. The simplicity of this piece of advice is its key: "Don't break the law and you won't get shot."

When black people can't seem to follow this simple advice that has worked for them, white people are just incredulous. They're frustrated. It's sooooo simple. Don't break the law and you won't have a problem. If only black people could follow simple directions. The implication is that if you weren't guilty, you wouldn't get shot. Sure, the death penalty is supposed to be for those tried and convicted of heinous, premeditated capital murder, but let's not get bogged down in details.

This conveniently omits all the people who were doing nothing wrong, who broke no laws and still got shot. Just a small sampling:

1. John Crawford, shot while holding a toy BB gun in a Walmart

2. Akai Gurley, shot while walking in his own apartment building's stairwell

3. Tamir Rice, a child shot while playing outside in the park

So, clearly, not everyone who gets shot is breaking the law. But if you *are* breaking the law, does that mean you should get shot? I guess it depends on which law you are breaking. Police apologists will cite the most extreme examples of this—people pointing guns at cops. Now, mind you, many of these cases are ones in which the only evidence of the gun being pointed at a cop is the cop's testimony that it happened.

But many police shootings don't happen after guns are pointed. Let's look at some laws that people broke that got them shot:

1. A broken taillight—Philando Castile got shot after he got pulled over for a "broken taillight."

2. Missing front plate—Samuel DuBose got shot after being pulled over for a missing front plate.

3. Not wearing a seat belt—Levar Jones got shot after being pulled over for not buckling up.

4. Resisting arrest—Resisting arrest is like irritable bowel syndrome. Irritable bowel syndrome is this catch-all for when your butt hurts; maybe you should stop eating neon junk food, or maybe it's some kind of problem with the bacteria in your gut. Nobody knows. But everybody knows your butt hurts. It's the same with resisting arrest—nobody likes getting arrested, so everyone's going to resist it somewhat. Police have wide latitude to decide if you are resisting arrest—it's whatever they say it is.

So, clearly breaking some of these laws shouldn't be a capital offense. But given that almost any breaking of the law can be a capital offense for black people, I'm going to have to reiterate white advice on this one: don't break the law.

Don't break any law. And I mean *any* law. Not speeding, not having a broken taillight, not even the law of attraction. Matter of fact, stay away from anything with "law" in it. Whatever has a law in it, don't break it. The laws of nature, the laws of gravity—you ever seen a black astronaut? Not many. Because trust me, if it has law in it, it will just fuck you up.

DON'T REACH FOR A WEAPON

"The term unarmed black man may be literally accurate, but it doesn't tell the whole story in most cases. In a number of cases, if the victim ended up being unarmed, it was certainly not for a lack of trying." —Tomi Lahren

It's common sense that if you pull a gun on a cop, they will shoot you. This is not hard to anticipate. Assuming you're not some kind of violent criminal, why do people still do this? Well, some of the people who were killed reaching for their guns didn't *know* that they were reaching for their guns.

Some people "reaching for their guns" were getting their wallets out or scratching an itch, or who knows what. They didn't mean to reach for their "gun"; they didn't even have a gun! But cops don't know that and are often looking for guns where there aren't any. To a cop, anything "might" be a gun.

GUNS:

- Your wallet
- Your license and registration
- Your phone
- That book you were reading
- A candy bar
- Anything that feels "gun"-like in the dark, when you're biased

DON'T REACH

So what to do if you are asked to reach for something? Don't. Don't reach. Declare yourself "not it." Let the cop do the reaching.

Even white girls know better nowadays. In Georgia, this cop pulled these two girls over. One was drunk. He was gonna take the other one to jail, so he says "Reach for your phone. You can use your phone to call somebody." But she wouldn't do it. She said that she didn't want to reach for her cell phone because she had seen "way too many videos" of people getting shot by cops. You know shit's bad when a white woman is scared of the police. Now either she's *really* woke or she has fucked a lot of black guys. "Jamal told me this is how you're supposed to act around cops. . . ."

Anyway, then the cop joked, "But you're not black. Remember, we only kill black people. Yeah. We only kill black people, right?" That cop was essentially forced to retire for telling a sarcastic joke, even though he was telling the truth. Isn't it ironic: you basically get fired for *joking* about shooting a black man, but *shooting* a black man—that's different.

But this girl had the right idea—be careful what you reach for.

THE PROBLEM WITH POCKETS

The trouble is, anywhere you might keep a gun is also a place you might keep a wallet or license. Pockets are convenient, but a safety hazard. Stop wearing stuff with pockets. Do you really need all that pocket change if you're dead?

SAFE BAGS

So, no pockets. If you're a man, maybe now is the time to buy one of those man purses so you don't have pockets to dip into—a murse might save your life. If you're a woman, maybe it's time get yourself a tiny purse, a clutch or something that doesn't seem as easy to pack heat in.

You know what I just realized? Bags are another problem. Guns can easily be stored in a backpack or a bag! Hell, movies always show some lady pulling a gun out of her purse. I don't remember a gun being pulled out of a murse, but times are changing.

BETTER YET, MAYBE DON'T CARRY ANYTHING

You're probably better off not carrying anything.

"License and registration, please."

"Sorry, Officer, but I don't carry that shit because I don't like reaching for things and getting shot."

DON'T REACH FOR A "WEAPON," EITHER

But let's say you're holding something or reaching for something that's definitely not a weapon. It's not a gun. It's not a knife. It's not a crossbow. It's not a weapon. Be careful: that might be a weapon.

A weapon is in the eye of the beholder. Think about some of the shit that people get fucked up with in some of those kick-ass kung fu movies: lunch trays, jump ropes, hot soup dumplings. Anything can be a weapon. Or think about James Bond: that guy has pens that shoot lasers and walking canes that are both an umbrella *and* a sword. That guy's bow tie is a ninja star. So cops are rightfully concerned that anything can be weaponized.

Better to not hold things. Holding things can be hazardous to your health.

YOU DON'T HAVE A GUN . . . YET

And of course if you get shot and killed, you might come to find out that you *did* have a gun. Once the police investigate what happened, it might be that they *find* a gun. It's incredible how often a gun is found after an investigation when previously there wasn't any gun.

In St. Louis, Officer Jason Stockley was acquitted of shooting Anthony Lamar Smith in 2011 after he said, "We're killing this motherfucker." Even though the judge let him off, the prosecution alleged that he put a gun in the car. A different cop on the scene had said that he didn't see a gun and somehow this gun appeared after Stockley went back and forth to his car. Never mind that the gun didn't have any of Smith's DNA on it—it had only Stockley's DNA—the judge ruled that it wasn't plausible to believe that a dope dealer wouldn't have a gun. So it's not plausible to believe that there's no way a dope dealer wouldn't have a gun? This comes as a big surprise to pharmacists. Watch out, CVS.

There are many, many cases where cops planted guns after the fact to justify a shooting. So even death won't prevent you from getting shot for carrying a gun.

SUMMARY

Don't reach for a weapon. Or for anything: don't reach for your license, don't reach for the stars, your dreams, whatever. Stay away from it. Just remember:

- Anything can be a gun.
- Don't carry anything.
- Don't carry anything that can carry anything.
- Anything can be a weapon.
- Even if you follow these rules, you might have a "gun." So it's important to be vigilant even in death: don't even carry a gun posthumously.

STUFF WHITE PEOPLE SAY

Law & Order Fan #1: "But, DL: What about 'black-on-black crime?'"

Weirdly, "black-on-black" crime is a reason a lot of white people are scared of black people. Why are white people worried about black-on-black crime? Do you see "white" in that sentence? It doesn't make sense.

Except that if you keep hearing about "black-on-black" crime, it gives you an excuse to fear black people. Society parrots back to you that black people are inherently to be feared. After a police shooting, people say, "Well, it was a high-crime area." They mean that this dude got shot because all the black people there must be dangerous.

People like to point to a report that says 90 percent of black people who are murdered are murdered by other black people. But the same report also says that 83 percent of white people who are murdered are murdered by white people. Turns out that most people are murdered by people they know! Turns out that there's no point in worrying about black-on-black crime, just like nobody's worried about white-on-white crime. Crime is crime.

To me, the idea of "black-on-black crime" is more dangerous to black people than the word "nigger" ever was. Because it's a call to arms that basically says that we have this urgent situation. Black people are killing black people and we have to do something about it before anything else. It's used as a tool for inaction and to discredit Black Lives Matter, as if Black Lives Matter is ignoring a problem that needs to be solved before we can even talk about police violence. You even have black people like Ray Lewis and Fox Sports' Jason Whitlock toeing this line. Just because one bad thing is happening, that doesn't mean you shouldn't try to solve another. Fox News is just using it as an excuse not to deal with police violence. It's a way to paint all black people as violent, as if they deserve violence.

It's like if a bank got robbed all the time, right? The police can't pull up and start pulling money from that bank just because it got robbed all the time. When the police break up a sex-trafficking ring, you can't go, "Hey, this girl fucked a lot, so let's fuck her again." They can't do that. But that makes sense when it's black people? "These niggas are used to it." Police violence against black people is okay because black people are already victims of violence?

During the campaign, Trump kept talking about "Chicago" and how he was going to bring in the National Guard if they couldn't solve their crime problem. Okay. So obviously, Chicago is a very violent city. But it's also one of the cities with the highest unemployment rates for black men in the country (14.2 percent in 2016, according to the Economic Policy Institute, compared with 8.4 percent nationwide). The notion that you would tell people to put their guns down when they don't have any opportunity or a job is absurd. Black-on-black crime is more about proximity than about any kind of particular moral failure. It's about poor people with limited resources who can't access education and jobs. And then you add in liquor stores and drugs and guns; it's not really that difficult to ascertain what the outcome of that would be. Broke people kill broke people. People with no hope, with only despair; they kill a lot of people.

So "Chicago" is just a code word. They didn't say a fucking thing about Chicago when Laquan McDonald was shot by the police in 2014 and the police stonewalled the investigation for months. Why didn't they want anyone to see the tapes? Because they shot a dude with a knife for no reason, that's why. Eight fucking cops and they can't disarm a guy with a knife in the middle of the highway?

And when a police officer is frightened of a black guy, it means they are scared whether they had an experience with that black person or not. They can't differentiate between a good guy and a bad guy. They're scared of all black people because of something they saw on some TV screen about a shooting a thousand miles away. That to me is classic racism.

So let's face it: White people don't care about violent crime in "Chicago." They love violent crime in Chicago. They love it because it's their favorite bogeyman: "black-on-black crime."

4

YOU HAVE TO UNDERSTAND: COPS ARE SCARED

"I fired my gun at Mr. Crutcher because I was fearing for my life."

—Officer Betty Jo Shelby, testifying why she shot Terence Crutcher

In this, and so many other cases, an innocent black person gets shot because the cop is frightened. They have a scary job! They are put in a lot of weird situations and often have to deal with angry people. It's not all giving old ladies directions or busting people for going 50 in a 45 zone.

Being a cop can be dangerous. But it's not *always* dangerous. Even the cops who aren't white supremacists can misinterpret the threat at hand. And some are like Barney Fife, small men in a big uniform. Some have a serious case of the yips and are just one scary moment away from shooting someone.

Juries are buying this narrative, too. Betty Jo Shelby was let off for killing Terence Crutcher because she was scared. Officer Jeronimo Yanez was let off for killing Philando Castile because he was scared. Officer Timothy Loehmann was let off for killing Tamir Rice because he was scared.

When you talk to white people, "being scared" is more than enough to excuse a cop shooting someone. Sure, they got a gun, a dog, and a helicopter. So if they're afraid, I bet you're fucking afraid, too. But now isn't the time to worry about *you* being scared. I'm trying to get you not shot!

WHAT'S SCARY ABOUT BLACK PEOPLE?

White people have always been scared of black people. And when a black person gets shot, there's usually a sense from the commentary of white people that because the cop was scared, they deserved it. It doesn't have to be something the victim specifically did to make them afraid at the time, because you have to understand there's a *historical* fear. And so history lets the cop act with a heightened sense of danger when it comes to policing black people.

1. Black People Live in "Bad" Neighborhoods

Cops are scared because they are dealing with people in "bad" neighborhoods. This is one of the Right's favorite dog whistles: emphasize "black on-black" crime. So because of the racist housing policies that have segregated people of color into "bad neighborhoods," *anyone* who lives in that neighborhood is "bad" and dangerous.

2. Black People Are Strong!

Take a look at how Officer Darren Wilson described Michael Brown in his grand jury testimony: "When I grabbed him the only way I can describe it is I felt like a five-year-old holding on to Hulk Hogan. Hulk Hogan, that's how big he felt and how small I felt just from grasping his arm."

This fear of black people's strength goes back at least to the bad old days of slavery. During the height of the lynching era, news stories were full of "black brutes" terrorizing white people. In the 1980s and '90s, there were the stories of "superpredators" hopped up on crack and angel dust. Recently there was even a paper where researchers showed that white patients were more likely to receive painkillers than black patients; even doctors demonstrate unconscious bias and entrenched ideas about biological differences between races. Another study found that whites thought blacks were more likely to have superhuman abilities like enhanced strength and endurance. I'm serious!

I blame Marvel Comics. Look at the black superheroes: Black Panther? Black Panther is strong as fuck. Who does that help? And Luke Cage? Luke Cage is bulletproof. Marvel Comics and Netflix are gonna get a lot of people killed! Nobody wants a bulletproof nigga. Even niggas don't want a bulletproof nigga. When I shoot a nigga, I want him to lie down; I don't want him to stand. I don't want white people to see Luke Cage and go, "See—I knew these niggas won't be stopped with just one shot. It's like *The Walking Dead*: you gotta shoot 'em in the head!"

Super strength, being bulletproof: that's all fine for white superheroes. But for black superheroes: fuck jumping over a building or being faster than a speeding bullet. Luke Cage can keep his big bike chain or whatever the hell. The superpower that black people need is the *ability to have white people believe them*. That's what I want. The ability to have white people go, "That nigga's telling the truth."

Here, I jotted down an idea:

Marvel: call me up if you want to license some of this shit. I see a comic-book franchise ahead.

3. Black People Are "Different"

A lot of white people find black people unfamiliar and make assumptions based on stereotypes. The fact that with no evidence so many people questioned if Obama was born in this country goes to show how white people find black people "different" and not "one of us." When people refer to "real Americans" and so-called middle America, they're talking about white folks who live in predominantly white areas—like in a fucking cornfield somewhere in Iowa. Never mind that black people had been pouring their sweat and blood into American soil long before most white people's ancestors showed up here: twenty blacks arrived in Virginia in 1519, the year before the *Mayflower* landed. And most slaves were brought over from Africa before 1808, even before the end of slavery in 1865. That means most African Americans' ancestors arrived decades if not centuries before the waves of Irish, German, Italian, Jewish, and Polish immigration. Still, most everything in America is geared toward white people. American culture is presumed "white."

Forget about the fact that white people listen to a lot of hip-hop. Forget about the racial makeup of the sports teams that white people like. A jittery white cop is going to look at a black person as "different" and scary.

LET'S WORK WITH THE RACISM

Take the most stereotypical image of a black person a racist cop could have: a gangbanger in a lowrider, smoking a blunt, listening to loud rap music while twirling his piece. If that's how a racist cop sees black people, let's work *with* that racism and reverse-engineer it to put the cop at ease. Cops get spooked so easily; let's make us less scary!

If you're getting pulled over by a cop, let's see if we can make sure you're not playing into racist stereotypes.

Racist Stereotype	Alternative
Drive a lowrider, pimped-out ride	Drive a sensible minivan with great mileage. (Avoid any car with a 0–60 time of less than 10 seconds.)
Listen to rap music	Listen to Bach's Suite Number 3 in C Major, featuring Yo-Yo Ma. (Really, playing music from the past 100 years is a risk.)
Smoke weed, have a stash in car	Suck on butterscotch, have a bag of Werther's Originals in car
Gun under the seat	Blue Lives Matter bobblehead on dash

SUMMARY

Understanding that cops are scared of black people is one of the first steps to not getting shot. Knowing their biases can help police-shoot-proof you:

- If you're in a black neighborhood, you are in a bad neighborhood.
- If you're black, you're strong, maybe too strong.
- If you're black, you're different.

Now that you know what the stereotypes are, you can work *with* them to make yourself less shootable!

STUFF WHITE PEOPLE SAY

Blue Lives Matter Guy #4: "But, DL: Cops have a hard job! You can't blame everything on them."

Cops *do* have a hard job.

And in all fairness, putting police officers in a position where they have to be counselors and psychologists and negotiators isn't right. Most of the time, people call the police for help, not a bullet. So it's unfair to put them in a situation where they have to be all things to all people.

But that is the gig! And if you wanted to fix that situation, you wouldn't fix it just by giving cops more bulletproof shit.

You don't fix it by giving them tanks and riot gear. You don't do therapy through bulletproof glass.

And why is it that working to end racial bias in the police department is viewed as an attack on police?

The thing is that most of the people arrested in this country are white. Most of the people who shoot cops aren't black. So what is it that makes cops think and act extra aggressively toward black people? Hmm, what could it be if it's not race?

There are tens of thousands of traffic stops that do not end in fatalities. But out of all the stops that *do* end in fatalities, the largest number of them percentage-wise happen to black people. And, as we noted above, that's irrespective of whether they're poor or rich. The poor get shot more than anybody else, but rich *black* people—they get shot more than their neighbors do.

So, okay, you say, why focus on the horrifically unsuccessful stops when there are thousands, maybe hundreds of thousands of successful police stops in this country—hundreds of thousands that don't result in death. Fine. Airplanes take off millions of times a year. But if an airline has a crash—even one—we all know something went terribly wrong. So, despite all the successful flights, we still thoroughly investigate the tragedy to try to fix what went wrong so that people will feel safe.

It's the same thing. When a police shooting happens, something went terribly wrong. Unless you believe that's the way things are supposed to go. It wouldn't be okay to say, "Well, planes are dangerous, sometimes they crash!" We've gotten really good at making sure planes don't crash, because people want them to be safe. We don't say #AllPlanesMatter.

And another thing: when a plane crashes, you say something went wrong with the *plane*, not the passengers. You don't say, "The passengers must have done something." And you have a black box recording the flight data so we know what happened. We don't let the fucking pilots turn off the black box. "Well, we had a black box, but they turned it off before the plane crashed." No. There's one button: record.

In America, when something goes wrong, we fix it. We allocated millions of dollars to eradicate the Zika virus. Remember Ebola? Not one person died of Ebola in the continental United States. Not one. But $35 million was allocated by the end of 2014. Eight hundred fifty unarmed people get killed by the police and we worry about a mosquito.

To not work on this problem is to admit we collectively think that it's actually *not* a problem. When it comes to black people, most white people would never say this out loud, but they believe this is the way the system was designed to work. It's supposed to be like this.

5

DO BE AN ANGEL

"He looked up at me and had the most intense aggressive face. The only way I can describe it, it looks like a demon, that's how angry he looked."

—Darren Wilson's description of Michael Brown

If you have a criminal record, it's okay you got shot. That seems to be the attitude of white people to police violence. It might be a little extreme; overkill, if you will. But basically okay.

White people think that bad things only happen to bad people. *They* were good people and the nice policeman let them off with a warning. See: it pays to be nice! If you got shot by the police, *you* must have done something bad to deserve it.

So if you want justice, be sure you're an angel.

POLICE INVESTIGATIONS

If you do get shot by the police, you'd better believe there will be an investigation—of *you*, anyway. Hope you don't have a criminal record! When a black suspect is shot, the media and their accomplices in the police department will be sure to make that public. Everyone will know that you "were no angel." That's apparently justification enough for police brutality, even killing. "See, he was a bad dude—you can understand how he might get shot." Bad dudes get what they deserve.

So Michael Brown deserved to die because he robbed a convenience store.

So Eric Garner deserved to die because he sold illegal cigarettes.

So Alton Sterling deserved to die because he had been previously arrested for domestic battery.

With victims of police brutality, they'll always try to blame the victim, as if the victim deserved to die. This shit's been going on forever. In the early 1990s in Detroit, the police beat Malice Green over the head with a flashlight, killing him. At trial, the police had a coroner testify that Malice died of heart failure because of his prior drug use. Okay, so it's his fault that he's not strong enough to take an ass whooping?

COPS ARE PRESUMED TO BE ANGELS

They don't do that with cops, though. Cops are assumed to be heroes. In July 2016, five Dallas cops were killed in an attack that had the right yelling "#BlueLivesMatter" as loudly as ever. Killing cops is terrible, of course. But are they all *presumed* heroes? One of the cops who was killed was described as a "gentle giant." Isn't that nice? To be a big, cuddly gentle giant. Makes you just want to curl up in his lap and get a big fucking hug. It's a little different description than of similarly sized Michael Brown before he was killed (Officer Darren Wilson: "the only way I can describe it is I felt like a five-year-old holding on to Hulk Hogan").

In any case, after Officer Lorne Ahrens was killed, he was described as a "gentle giant" and a family man; gushing news reports eulogized this fallen hero. And I'm not saying it's right to shoot a cop. But it turns out that this gentle giant was fond of Thor's hammer, the Iron Cross, and a bunch of other white supremacy symbols. A big hero? Maybe more like a massive racist. The Jolly White Nationalist.

Did that mean he deserved to be shot? Of course not. But neither did Michael Brown deserve to be shot for shoplifting. It's not relevant. White shooting victims are heroes until proven otherwise. Black shooting victims had better be squeaky clean or people will say they "got what they deserved."

LIST OF MINOR OFFENSES AND THE
TRUMPED-UP CHARGES

Of course, even if you are squeaky-clean, they'll find something to make you look bad. Since it's important that a black victim was justifiably killed, here's how it gets twisted after the fact to make it seem okay:

Action	Black Shooting Victim	White Shooting Victim
Drinking in public	"Alcoholic"	"Wine connoisseur"
Smoking weed	Drug user	Fair-trade entrepreneur
Got angry	"Demon"	Independent-minded
Talked back	Verbally assaulted	Gave a piece of his mind

And of course if you don't have a criminal record, that doesn't mean you're out of the woods. Just make sure that no one in your vicinity has done any criminal activity that you could be associated with. Because if they can't find dirt on you, they'll look into your loved one's history.

Tamir Rice was an innocent twelve-year-old boy, so the *Cleveland Plain Dealer* looked into his father's history instead. They reported that Tamir's father had a history of violence against women, to provide context—or in one Cleveland reporter's words, "a frame of reference." Now what the fuck Tamir's father's record has to do with police shooting him as he played in the park, I don't know. What "context" does that provide, when Tamir was a victim? Here's the context: it's important to make sure that every police shooting looks justified.

AND YOU'LL LOOK LIKE SHIT, TOO

If a white person gets shot, you know they run the sweetest picture of the victim from his or her high school yearbook or a picture of them on the beach somewhere. But for black folk, they're not running the nice smiley picture of you. Come on. You know that they're running the scariest-Negro-they-can-find picture. It's like a black person before and after:

You, before the shooting:

You, after the shooting:

One more time. Before:

After:

Damn, they can make anyone look like shit.

SUMMARY

Don't give anyone a reason to shoot you. I'm not saying you have to be perfect, but it helps.

- If you can't be an angel, at least be a choirboy. If you can't be a choirboy, at least get your record expunged.
- If you're perfect, make sure that your family and friends are perfect, too.
- If the media can make me look bad . . . shit. You're fucked.

LET'S MEET SOME SHERIFFS!

Not all cops are just cops—some are a special category: sheriffs! Sheriffs are like modern-day cowboys, a John Wayne fantasy come to life. White people just love their sheriffs. There's just something about the word "sheriff" that tickles white people's fancy and makes them feel like they're still living in the Old West or something. The

tough-talking, horse-ridin', cowboy-hat-wearin' sheriffs
are still with us. The original good old boys, the original law-
and-order types that like to kick ass and take names, they
seem like they're from another age. One before police reform, civilian oversight, or fair treatment. Sheriffs can dole
out justice as they see fit, even if their vision is skewed. Let's
saddle up and meet a few of these modern-day cowboys:

Sheriff David Clarke

Sheriff David Clarke: A rare black man willing to go
on Fox News and toe the line, Sheriff Clarke is a tough-
talking lawman who white people love. A black cowboy?
Neat. Up until recently, he was the sheriff of Milwaukee
County, where he liked to rail against Black Lives Matter,

even though at least four people have died in his county jail since 2016. This guy is nutty. In an editorial titled "This Is a War and Black Lives Matter Is the Enemy," he wrote: "We as a people need to declare that we stand with rule of law, and not with the false tales of the revolutionary Marxist forces, who most recently have rebranded themselves from Occupy Wall Street to Black Lives Matter." Um, what?

Luckily, he has stepped down to "pursue other opportunities." It seemed like one of those opportunities was supposed to be a position with the Trump administration's Homeland Security Department, but now it seems like that offer ain't happening. Though who knows, maybe Omarosa's departure provides an opening.

Sheriff Joe Arpaio

Sheriff Joe Arpaio: One of the most famous sheriffs around, Sheriff Joe Arpaio was the recipient of a rare preemptive presidential pardon. Why did he need a pardon? Because his form of justice was ignoring court orders to stop violating people's rights. This guy was pardoned by Trump despite some truly despicable behavior.

He ran "Tent City" in Arizona—an outdoor prison facility for people he suspected of being illegal aliens that he himself called a "concentration camp." You know you're on the wrong side when you run your own concentration camp. That doesn't go well. He made inmates wear pink underwear and eat green bologna sandwiches. And he got sued.

Fox News was full of defenders of the pardon, saying, "What about all the people who have lost their lives to illegal immigrants who shouldn't be here?" Explain to me how one thing relates to the other? How can you defend his behavior? This is a bad guy. Another example: his officers handcuffed a pregnant inmate for suspected ID theft, had the courtesy to uncuff her during her actual C-section delivery, but then slapped the restraints back on as soon as she got to the recovery room.

How does a pregnant woman threaten law-abiding citizens? That's what I don't get. A baby is dangerous? This baby might be an alien, but it's not the baby from *Alien* running around chomping people. I mean, babies are aliens.

But it's not that baby. I mean, everybody saw *Alien*, right? That is a fucking scary movie. Who wasn't freaked out by that alien baby?

But what was I saying? I don't understand how people who defend Sheriff Joe Arpaio can say, "My child was killed by an illegal alien, so I'm gonna make grown men walk around in pink underwear." That's gonna make someone not murder somebody? People will stop trying to come into our country because of the bologna sandwiches? I don't understand the logic.

6

DON'T DRIVE LIKE A SUSPECT

> "When we make a stop, it's not based on race or gender or anything of that nature. It's based on probable cause that some law is being broken, whether it's traffic or otherwise."
>
> **—Lincoln Hampton, spokesman for the Illinois State Police**

So many police shootings start when someone gets pulled over by the cops. Philando Castile was pulled over 49 times in 13 years. And yet white people drive all over the place without getting stopped. So how do you avoid being pulled over by the cops? What secrets can we learn from white people?

Okay—I know and you know that a lot of the reason black people get pulled over is simply DWB—driving while black. In state after state, data shows that police officers are more likely to pull over black drivers than white ones. Experts disagree about whether that shows that cops are racially profiling people or that the cars black people drive look suspicious. I think we understand that cops are racially profiling, but that's a bit harder to fix. So . . . let's fix our cars!

HAVE A NICE CAR

It seems like half the time black people get pulled over, it is because of a broken taillight. Why? Bad car maintenance is getting people killed!

How do you keep a car maintained? Well, sure: have money. That helps a lot. But even if you don't have money, you can do a minimal amount of preventative maintenance to keep your car good-looking enough to not get pulled over.

Even though it's basically the whitest radio show ever, black people could benefit from listening to *Car Talk* on NPR. Click and Clack, the Tappett brothers, hand out car advice to listeners in the corniest way possible, but heck, they could be lifesavers.

Auto maintenance for white people starts with the engine. Auto maintenance for black people starts with the taillight. The cops won't pull you over for a fucked-up engine, but they will for a broken taillight. A broken taillight is basically a broken car to you.

Other frequent targets for cops: burned-out headlights, broken windshields, expired tags, and missing front license plates. If you've got a junky car, you'll recognize that list. And look: you know you're really dark when your windows aren't tinted and they think they are. You've done enough with the dark. Stay away from it.

It's important to have a nice car. But maybe not too nice a car. Too nice a car can seem suspicious. So don't go overboard.

DRIVE RIGHT

Another reason a lot of black drivers get pulled over is that they "don't obey the traffic laws." They improperly switch lanes, for instance. Or they are driving too fast. Or like in Florida recently when state attorney Aramis Ayala was pulled over by the Orlando Police Department because she had a, um, her tags, well, the, um, tags came back empty? And her window tint was, it was just weird. Or something.

So be sure to observe all traffic laws. Be sure to signal if you need to change lanes. Better yet, don't change lanes. Drive straight. Don't turn. Turning can get you in trouble. Everywhere you go has to be straight forward. And so, if you've got to visit somebody and you have to make a left turn, they're off your list. Desperate times call for desperate measures. Stay straight!

Oh shit, now I sound homophobic. We can worry about the gays later. Oh shit, they're here. Well, it's better than being shot. An angry tweet from GLAAD—I'll take that over a bullet from a cop.

DON'T HAVE TOO MANY PEOPLE IN YOUR CAR

Don't have more than three people in your car. Yes, there are seats for at least five people in even the smallest car. But if you have too many people in your car, you will attract the attention of the police. There's something about large gatherings of black people that they don't like.

HAVE A WHITE FRIEND

If you're going out, bring along a friend. If you have a couple of choices, bring along a white guy. A white dude is helpful to vouch for you in case you get pulled over. Carrying around a white guy might be even more important than carrying around your driver's license. You might not want to bring your white friend, but he's like a fire extinguisher—break seal in case of emergency.

Attention men: please note that I said bring along a white *guy*. We're not talking about a white woman. That could put you in a worse situation. And never, ever let these things come together at the same time:

1. Well dressed

2. Nice-looking

3. Black body

4. Nice car

5. White woman

A well-dressed, nice-looking black dude with a nice car and a white woman: that's a problem. You can have two of those five things, maybe three of those five things, but you can't have five of those five things. That's suspicious as fuck. Unless you're an NBA ballplayer and your team has just won the championship, in which case all bets are off. But if you aren't one of the three guys in the entire world that has happened to, you're in trouble.

It's like those symptoms you look at on WebMD that scare the shit out of you and convince you that you've got a horrible disease. You can have one or two of those symptoms, but if you have them all—shit, you have lupus. If I were you, I'd get a cream for that rash. But I digress.

DON'T BE LOST

Never be lost. Black people cannot get lost. Always know where you are. Always know where you're going. Getting lost is different for white people. When Christopher Columbus got lost, that motherfucker got America. When black people get lost, somebody dies or goes to jail.

If you're black, you've got to be organized. Always know where you're going and what time you left to get there. You want to have your route planned so you're on the road the shortest amount of time. Get friendly with Google Maps. Remember, the shortest distance between two points is a straight line; if you're going straight like I told you, you won't have a problem.

And whenever possible, stay on streets named after famous black people, like Martin Luther King Boulevard or Malcolm X Boulevard. Or in a pinch, streets named after Mexicans or whatever. Caesar Chavez Boulevard is still safer than John C. Calhoun Street. And if you're on Robert E. Lee Boulevard, get the fuck out.

Having Trouble with the Po-Po?

Are you like me, always getting pulled over by the police for driving while black and then getting jammed up on some made-up bullshit? Maybe you've tried everything:

- Crimestoppers bumper stickers
- Police Benevolent Association window decals
- Being polite
- Complying with police orders

And you're still having trouble. Even I, D. L. Hughley, can run into trouble. One time, Los Angeles County sheriff Lee Baca gave me his business card in case I ever got in a jam. I don't think I'll be able to take him up on his offer, since he's in prison for lying to federal officials in a jail corruption scandal. But even if I could, there's no guarantee that he could help before I was being arrested for something. Every black person needs a powerful solution.

Well, it sounds like we need: Po-Po-Potpourri!

If you want to keep your car fresh, it's good to have an air freshener. But get one that'll help you if you get in trouble. White people might want Vanilla or Autumn Breeze or some other Yankee Candle bullshit. Potpourri: that's not for you. You need Po-Po-Potpourri!

How many times have you been arrested because cops "smelled marijuana"? How many times does this mysterious smell occur even when there is no weed in the car. Don't give cops a reason to arrest you or worse! Get Po-Po-Potpourri!

Po-Po-Potpourri is the only air freshener that rids the air of the invisible smell of marijuana that only appears in the police report.

Po-Po-Potpourri Will Set You Free

7

IF YOU DO GET SHOT, DON'T RUSH TO JUDGMENT

"An exhaustive Department of Justice investigation exonerated Wilson of any wrongful conduct. A similar thing happened in the case of Trayvon Martin. At trial, his killing was found to be done in self-defense, notwithstanding the rush to judgment the other way. The moral: We need to hear both sides."
—Richard A. Epstein, "The Shooting of Blacks by Cops and the Rush to Judgment," *Newsweek,* **July 13, 2016,** **http://www.newsweek.com/shooting -blacks-cops-and-rush-judgment-479746**

What if you or someone else you know does get shot? This book is about not getting shot, but sometimes even a book can't help you avoid the consequences of systemic racism and bias. If you do get shot, white people want to make sure you don't rush to judgment. After all, not all cops are bad!

DON'T RUSH TO JUDGMENT

Nobody *wants* to rush to judgment. But to black people, if an armed man has shot an unarmed man, there *has already been* a rush to judgment. So what authorities are actually saying is that they don't want there to be a rush to judgment on *their* rush to judgment.

Two wrongs don't make a right

If a cop was a little too quick to judge and his judgment was final—that is, fatal—well, that doesn't mean you should be like him, minus the firearm: two wrongs don't make a right. What did Jesus say? "Judge not lest you be judged"? "Let he who is without sin cast the first stone," although I wouldn't because that is assault with a deadly weapon and you might get shot doing it.

So let's not rush to judge the rush to judge. Let's be patient!

Don't judge a book by its cover

Remember how boring you thought Steve Harvey's book was going to be? Bad example. But most of the time, judging a book by its cover is wrong. Every few months, white people trot out a new title in a series called *Cops Keep Killing People*. Each new release has the latest tragic scene on the cover. It sure seems to be the same book recycled over and over, but please don't form a judgment until you read all five hundred pages. Maybe this time the story will end differently and the cops will be the hero!

First impressions are not always correct

That's the essence of being profiled: judging someone on first impressions. So again, you are being asked to do better than the cop who pulled you over for the "broken taillight." Don't you go around profiling all cops!

WAIT FOR ALL THE FACTS TO COME IN

"Let's wait for all the facts to come in."

Why not? There'll be a months-long investigation, so why not wait for all the facts to come in? Then, once you have all the facts, you can see if you think there was a good reason for the cops to have shot you.

The investigation might include an internal report, investigated by other officers. These internal investigations vary from place to place, but the systems are often like those in Ferguson, where the Department of Justice found that "[p]olice supervisors and leadership do too little to ensure that officers act in accordance with law and policy, and rarely respond meaningfully to civilian complaints of officer misconduct."

Or they might be like the Cleveland Police Department, where investigators told the Justice Department "that they intentionally cast an officer in the best light possible when investigating the officer's use of deadly force."

Or it might include a grand jury. Under pressure, prosecutors have started empaneling more special grand juries to investigate police-related deaths. Of course, these grand juries hardly ever indict police officers. Maybe they are still waiting for the facts to come in.

A JURY OF YOUR PEERS

If you're really lucky, there will be a jury trial like in the 2015 Walter Scott case in South Carolina. He ran away, and an officer shot him in the back. That's not an opinion. There was a tape of the officer shooting him as Walter Scott ran away, and throwing his Taser down near the body to implicate the victim. And then the cop falsified the police report. All that was fully investigated and murder charges were brought. See, the system works!

Of course, that first jury still didn't convict him. Because it's gotta be hard to find twelve white people in South Carolina who don't hate black people. Sorry, my mistake—it wasn't an all-white jury: there was one black dude. Still, it's gotta be hard. After the state trial, it took the feds to step in before justice was served, and in December 2017 the officer was sentenced to twenty years in federal prison.

IF YOU'RE LUCKY, A WHITE PERSON WILL GET SHOT

The bottom line is, too few white people have seen a black person killed by the police where they didn't feel in some way they deserved it. There's a presumption of innocence that's given to police that's almost unexplainable. It doesn't matter what you see or what you hear: all the cop has to do is say, "I was afraid."

But sometimes, if you're lucky, the police fuck up and kill a white person. As I write this, just yesterday, the Minneapolis police killed a white woman. Worse, she was someone's fiancée. Even worse still, she was blond. And as if that weren't bad enough, she was Australian—we all know how lovable Australians are. That *Crocodile Dundee* guy was hilarious. The only way Chris Hemsworth could be cuter is if he was a koala bear.

If they're killing white, blond-haired Australian women, we don't have a chance. What if Nicole Kidman is next?

Or maybe we *do* have a chance. Usually it takes just such a killing to get people focused on why the police are so trigger-happy. It's one thing if a black dude gets shot, quite another if the cops are shooting blond ladies from Down Under. Oh, did

I mention she was a *yoga instructor*? That's just about the least shootable white person you could imagine.

If the police are that out of control, who's next? Quilters? Elementary school librarians? Optometrists?

Immediately after this one shooting, the Minneapolis police chief resigned and an investigation was started. Maybe a tragic killing that white people can relate to will get them to be serious about reforming the police. But let's not rush to judgment on that!

SUMMARY

If you do get shot, don't rush to judgment! If you're black, there's probably a very good reason for why you got shot.

- Don't you rush to judge the one who rushed to judge you.
- Be patient; don't judge a book by its racist, oppressive cover.
- Any police shooting is bound to be investigated, so wait for all the facts to be known and dismissed.

In the end, it might be that white people think you deserved to be shot. But if you're lucky, the police will start shooting even the most lovable white people and we'll finally get some reforms!

STUFF WHITE PEOPLE SAY

Well-Meaning White Guy #2: "But, D.L.: Police departments are trying to reform. Look at how they've started using body cameras in lots of departments. That's good, right?"

Here's the thing—if there's a police shooting, the authorities never let the public see the video until they've had a chance to review it. Which is weird to me, because it's our video. It's the public's video, right? Those are our tax dollars at work.

There's always a long delay before the police release the video, if they ever do. If the purpose of the body cam is to create transparency, then they should want to show the footage immediately. Right then. But they don't. What they want to do is to see it, make a story up, and then show it.

That's not transparency. They should get the tape, press play, and the police see it when we see it. That would be transparency. It's the public's video equipment.

Instead we get the video, if we do, after the police have looked at it, edited it, made sure the story works. In Baltimore, the police didn't even figure out how to do the editing right: they submitted videos showing them planting evidence. You don't put the outtakes in the movie. That's some shitty filmmaking. Are we shooting *Police Academy 8: Body Cams*? The police defense is that they were just re-creating finding drugs that they didn't get on camera. You know, take two.

So that's what we've got now: police who can plant evidence, cover it up, and then claim it was a reenactment. We didn't buy it so cops could make home movies.

"Oh, the lighting wasn't right. Do it again." It's not a fucking selfie!

"Oh, my eyes were closed." It's not for their YouTube channel.

"Let's do one where I bust down the door from a low-angle and then we dolly in to a tight close-up." We ain't making *America's Saddest Home Videos* here. Baltimore PD: *The Wire* was canceled.

A reenactment. Hard to believe that this is the department that killed Freddie Gray while in police custody. Their care in capturing necessary shots for their cinematic opus seems at odds with their lack of care in letting Gray bounce around in their van until he died of a spinal cord injury. Maybe the police forgot to tell us that the van was out scouting locations for their next big feature.

In Albuquerque, New Mexico, police shot and killed a

woman and then seem to have edited the body camera footage before uploading it. A former police department records keeper says that this fits a pattern of cover-ups on video footage by the police there. In a lawsuit filed over the shooting death of Mary Hawkes, her family alleges that video footage from the police officer who shot her is missing (due to a faulty cable, according to the officer who shot her) or incomplete due to editing after the fact.

So maybe we can't trust the police to provide the transparency on this. It could be that police officers are like eager little film majors, Spielberg wannabes, or maybe just D. W. Griffith. Or maybe it turns out that body cameras are another tool for the same old story we keep seeing—cops shooting people without cause. These body-cam videos are the worst kind of unwanted sequel.

POLICE DEPARTMENT OPERATIONS MEMORANDUM

SUBJECT: Body Camera Usage Guide

The police department has issued body cameras to all officers. In an effort to increase accountability and help with the training of our officers, the department has issued the following guidelines for body camera use:

1. With limited exceptions, officers are required to activate their body cams when responding to ALL calls. Limited exceptions include:

   • When you forget
   • When something weird is about to go down
   • When you might record something incriminating

2. Officers are required to obtain consent prior to recording interviews with crime victims. Except if they are trying to be "tricky" or if the crime victim is probably lying.

3. Officers may turn off cameras during conversations with witnesses who do not want to be on camera. Also, if they need to threaten or belittle.

4. Officers must provide a written statement explaining their decision to not record. Just make something up.

5. The department has policies to prevent data tampering, deleting, or copying. But don't worry, we'll only release footage if people get really pissed.

6. Training will be provided to all those being issued a body camera. But you understand that when we say

training, we mean not really a lot of training—just enough to make it seem like we give a shit.

As a general guideline, if something is about to happen that you don't want people to know about, make sure your camera is off. We can stonewall for only so long.

8

THE *REAL* WAY TO NOT GET SHOT BY THE POLICE

So you still haven't been shot! That's great. You're already benefiting from the advice of white people. My book is working.

   *

   *

   *

   *

   *

Wait a minute. You see that space up there? That's me patting myself on my back because I am saving lives. If I can save just one person with this book, then we're going to have shitty sales. I want to save *lots* of lives. What the heck, maybe you should buy a copy for a friend of yours to save his life, too.

But you niggers know this shit ain't for real, right? I mean, don't get fucking cocky because this shit is a comedy book. We're trying to have a little comedy with tragedy. But I'm about to tell you the *real* secret to not getting shot by the police. Ready?

The only way to not get shot by the police is . . . to be lucky as a motherfucker. That's it. You can read this book, you can follow all the advice of well-meaning white folk, you can live a good, safe life. You can do whatever. But the best way to not get shot is to be lucky as a motherfucker.

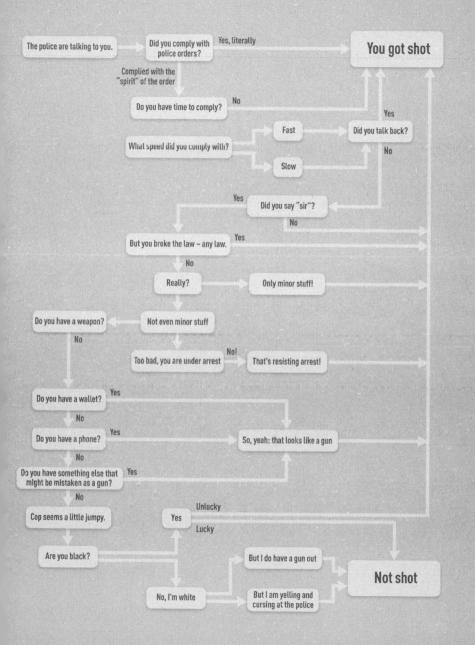

PART 2

HOW TO LOOK

Now that you're not dead, let's keep it that way. Being alive is a good look on you. But it's not enough. In this part, we're gonna get some great advice from white people about how we should look. Yes, believe it or not, we are going to hear some fashion tips from white people.

With so many cops scared of black people, it's important to find a way to put them at ease. First we'll take a look at how to dress less threatening. And it's very funny when white people claim they don't see color, because they're so good at describing us to the police. But is there a way to not "match the description"? There is! And finally, we'll get some advice about tattoos and how to do your hair Clarence Thomas–style.

Are you ready to find out how to look? Let's do it!

9

DON'T MATCH THE DESCRIPTION

"So I was sitting at an intersection and I see a white vehicle. I can't remember what kind of vehicle it was. . . . And I couldn't make out if it was a guy or girl I just knew that they were both African American."

Officer Yanez, describing why he pulled over Philandro Castile

Police pull black people over all the time because they "match the description." See what a fucking problem that is? I'm here to tell you, whatever you do, don't match the description.

Be taller, if you have to; shorter if you have to, fatter or skinnier, lighter or darker, longer or shorter hair; whatever you got to do. Just do not look like someone who did something.

LOOK UNIQUE

Some people are so unique looking that they never match the description. Have you ever heard of a crime committed by someone who looked like this:

If you get shot looking like that, you're shit out of luck. "I thought that giant clock was a gun!"

Have you ever seen anyone matching this description:

Okay, maybe:

But that's an exception.

In other words, if you've been looking to develop some questionable personal style, now's your chance. Wear a lot of crazy crap; it might save your life. You're trying to make sure that there's nobody out there that you might look like. If your style is so whack, you're never going to accidentally match the description.

DON'T LOOK UNIQUE

If you don't want to put in the energy to be totally unique, you can also go the other way. Be totally unremarkable. Have no distinguishing marks.

Think of a guy you don't remember and be like him. Got it?

Nice try—that guy was way too memorable—you remembered him! That's a guy you can remember. You're trying to be the most unremarkable black person you could ever be. You need to go deeper. You want to remember a guy you don't remember; that's the guy.

Maybe he's a guy you're not sure you even have ever met; he might not even exist. Think of what he's wearing—it's probably some kind of khaki pants but who can say? And he's got a shirt on? Maybe a blue shirt, maybe a tan shirt. Impossible to know. How tall was he? Average. Glasses—sometimes. That's your guy.

When you're shopping for clothes to be like this guy, you're really looking to pick clothes that anybody would choose. But be careful not to pick clothes that nobody would choose, because those are probably weird clothes.

DON'T BE SKETCHABLE

Here's a police sketch of the perpetrator. Do you look like him? If you do, don't go outside.

Sheridan Falls Police Department
1800 Witheron Ave
Sheridan Falls, NV
To be distributed to all deputies and superintendents
of Farral County

October 23
Case no. 4555300-01

WANTED
FOR HOMICIDE / ARMED ROBBERY

Suspect Description:
Sex: Male
Age: 31
Height: 5'10"
Weight: 180
Hair Color: Dark brown
Eye Color: Unknown

Wanted for homicide and armed robbery of Kosak Convenience Store on the corner of 34 and Higgins on the night of Sept. 24th. Suspect was last seen with a dark navy winter hat, blue jeans, and black sweatshirt.
If you have any information regarding this incident, call the Sheridan Falls Police Dept. Callers will remain anonymous.

W-203-01

All police sketches look the same.
They all have:

1. A bad attitude

2. The dude's head is a little squat

3. No forehead

4. Rabbit eyes

5. Goatee

6. Beanie

If you have a short little forehead and like to wear a beanie, you've got a problem because you already match the description. You're too sketchable. Not "sketchy"—*sketchable*.

DON'T LOOK LIKE YOUR YEARBOOK PICTURE

Have you ever noticed that every time a black guy commits a crime, they go back to his yearbook picture? And somehow he looks just like the kind of guy who would commit the crime he's accused of. He looks just like it. So whatever you do, don't look like you did in high school: guilty as hell.

Maybe Olan Mills should just arrest those people when they go in for their senior picture. As soon as your high school yearbook picture is developed, security arrests you.

"I didn't do anything!"

"You will."

Instead of that autumn leaves background, they give you cinder blocks. They hand you your booking number and make sure they have your profile and fingerprints. In your yearbook, you're "Most likely to do 10–20."

DON'T LET YOUR CAR MATCH THE DESCRIPTION

Before the cops even get to looking at you, they're looking for *cars* that "match the description." That's how half these shootings begin—the cops say they have a car that matches the description to some recent crime, then they pull someone over and they're already on edge. So if you want to be truly safe, you need a safe car.

The National Highway Traffic Safety Administration safety ratings: that's not us. Don't go looking at safety ratings; we're not talking about a Volvo. That's a safe car for white people. A safe car for black folks isn't a car that will help you in a crash. A safe car for black people is one that won't match the description. Here's the DL Traffic Safety Administration Top Safety Ratings:

#1: Oscar Mayer Wienermobile:

Admittedly, there may not be enough hot dogs to go around for all the black folks who need them.

#2: Smart Cars

Until criminals get wise to the easy parking and environmental benefits of using a smart car, these cars scream "Not guilty." Honorable mention: Teslas. White people figure that if you're conscientious enough to plug your car in at night, you're probably not the folks they're looking for. All cops would have to do to solve a crime would be to follow the extension cord.

#3: Golf Carts

White-collar criminals drive these, not the kind cops care about. Important note: though they may look similar, ATVs or four-wheelers do *not* accord the same protection.

If you commit a crime in a Wienermobile, you deserve all the time you get.

SUMMARY

Don't go getting yourself shot by "matching the description." There are so many ways to not look like someone who did something. There's always some guy who has done something and looking like him makes you more likely to get shot.

REMEMBER:

- Look totally unique.
- Or look just like that one guy you can never remember. Remember him? You don't? Perfect.
- If you love beanies or have a weird-shaped head, make sure you change it up to be less sketchable.
- Yearbook pictures can predict the future, so don't look like your guilty-looking yearbook picture.
- Drive a car that doesn't match the description—it might even be a good way to earn a little money on the side.

LET'S MEET
Jeff Sessions!

Jeff Sessions is a classic white person, whose lengthy service as a senator from the great state of Alabama was capped by an appointment as attorney general under President Trump. What a quintessential southern gentleman! His slow drawl and genteel manner are certainly charming.

Sessions was appointed attorney general despite a history of racially insensitive comments. You can understand that any southern gentleman of a certain age would make racial jokes and comments in good fun. Of course, Jeff Sessions denies it.

The only black assistant US attorney in Alabama at the time, Thomas Figures, testified that Sessions said the "NAACP, the Southern Christian Leadership Conference, Operation PUSH and the National Council of Churches were all un-American organizations teaching anti-American values" and that Sessions "thought those guys [the Ku Klux Klan] were OK until I learned they smoked pot."

Although these sorts of "jokes" got him rejected in 1986 when he was nominated by President Ronald Reagan for federal judge, they weren't enough to derail his confirmation in 2017 as Trump's attorney general. In 1986, these comments and his role in prosecuting voter registration advocates were too much. But not now! White people are back!

Jeff Sessions was also a key figure in the Trump campaign. Before most people thought Trump had a chance, Sessions was a big cheerleader for Trump. With the investigation into the Russian hacking scandal under way, he was asked in his confirmation hearing if he had ever met with Russian government officials. He said he had not. It was only later that his memory was jogged—oh, did they mean the *Russian ambassador* Sergey Kislyak? That kind of Russian government official? Well, yes, he had met him. But only two times. Or so.

Now, what can we expect out of his Justice Department? Well, he doesn't think the federal government needs to investigate police departments. The only people who are investigating anything about the police department right now is niggas. They're the only ones.

Among his first moves in office was to rescind an Obama-era directive to stop using private prisons. Sessions said the memorandum "impaired the bureau's ability to meet the future needs of the federal correctional system." Hmm, and who do you suppose are gonna be "meeting the needs" of these private prisons?

Private prisons are morally untenable, but the companies behind them were big donors to the Trump campaign. Many private prisons have an occupancy requirement that means that prisons have to be 80–100 percent full. You can actually bid for inmates. And what you want is young inmates with lengthy sentences that don't get sick. If you can get a cat in at age twenty, and he does twenty-five years, right at about the time he starts becoming a medical problem, you get rid of him. That way you keep your profits up.

That's the stuff that Jeff Sessions fights for: making sure we keep the police doing whatever the fuck they want and making sure there's plenty of space to lock the niggers up in.

LIKES: Mint juleps, private prisons, saying "I say, I say" before everything

DISLIKES: Testifying under oath, remembering things

10

HOW TO DRESS LESS THREATENING

"If you dress like a thug, people will treat you like a thug."

—Geraldo Rivera, talking about the death of Trayvon Martin

Dressing the wrong way can be dangerous! Just being out at night in a hoodie was enough to make Trayvon a threat. White people don't get how black people dress and sometimes it gets us killed. And white people can wear anything they want and it's fine. Is there a way to take a page from the white book and dress less threatening?

DON'T DRESS LIKE A THUG

Let's face it: black style has always been dangerous, from zoot suits to MC Hammer's parachute pants, white people clutch their pearls and worry about black fashion. They see it as foreign and, well, scary. Almost everything looks better on a black guy, but also more threatening. You can't help it. But being fly could make you die.

Have you ever felt threatened by the way white people dress? Even if you see a white guy in some kind of Ed Hardy skull T-shirt, it's hard to take them seriously. White people have perfected the art of nonthreatening dress: it's called Banana Republic. If you want to look totally nonthreatening, all you have to do is buy everything at the Banana Republic, or better yet call up Lands' End and say, "I'll take one of everything."

Fox News is always talking about black men looking like "thugs." Do-rags, sagging pants, and especially hoodies are fashion no-nos according to Fox. Wearing that sort of thing means you're advertising yourself to be a criminal. Obviously, it's wrong to say that every black man wearing a hoodie is a "thug." If I tried to tell you that every old white dude in khaki pants and a golf shirt is a racist, you wouldn't buy that argument.

My bad.

But the point is, you can't really tell that much from how someone dresses. There are probably as many black dudes dressed as thugs who *are* thugs as white people who are dressed like white supremacists who are white supremacists. But it's okay to dress one way, not the other.

But what am I trying to do here? Tell you how to dress with style the way I do? No, I'm trying to keep you safe and explaining how to dress the way white people like! So:

- No do-rags—try a cowboy hat or a derby instead.
- No sagging pants—white people hate sagging pants, which is weird because they don't have butts. They should like sagging pants.
- No hoodies—unless you follow the guidelines below.

HOW TO WEAR A HOODIE

Hoodies are a popular casual clothing item enjoyed by millions of Americans. From grandmas getting their steps in at the mall, to the young hipsters banging out some code in a Williamsburg café, hoodies are enjoyed by a variety of white people. And also some black people.

But did you know that black people are wearing them wrong? Crazy, right?

Wouldn't it be great to get a little white advice on how to wear them correctly? After all, white people have decades of experience with wearing hoods.

1. Hoods are DECORATIVE ONLY.

Even black people can catch a chill sometimes. So it would be tempting to view the hoods on hoodies as a "hat" that you could put up to keep your head warm. But that would be a mistake. A hoodie put up on top of the head makes it nearly impossible to tell if someone is black until their face is in view. This leads to a temporary disconnect: how can white people know how to treat you if they can't figure out if you're black?

2. Never wear headphones under your hoodie.

Let's say that a white person just has a "feeling" that you might be black. And naturally then they might want to ask you what you are up to, or why you are in the neighborhood you're in. How will you know what that white person is asking you if you can't hear them? It's probably pretty important, so you'll want to give this white person your full attention.

Also, if a white person is yelling at you but you don't know because you have headphones on, how will you know why they are upset with you? White people have short fuses and don't like to be ignored (see *police shootings*).

3. Hoodies are not evening wear.

Fashion has weird rules. Why are suit pants so short this season? Why isn't it okay to wear white after Labor Day when white people obviously love white things? Who can say? There's something about hoodies and black people that just makes them more suitable to daytime wear. And there's something about being out at night, in a hoodie, that lends itself to getting shot.

So let's just say that wearing hoodies at night is "out of style" for black people.

HOW TO DRESS WHITE

If you want to be safe, if you want to dress the white, I mean *right* way, try out some popular white outfits:

- Khakis and a nice button-down shirt
- Corduroy jacket with elbow patches, and heck let's throw in a pipe and fireplace, too
- Argyles

But fashion is a cruel mistress. Remember how everyone lost their minds when Obama wore a tan suit? You don't want to get it wrong and end up making things worse.

So what the fuck are black people supposed to wear? What article of clothing makes black people less threatening? What shop do we go to? They have a little-folk shop, for small people. They have Big & Tall for big people. They have Lane Bryant for bigger women, right? What do we have? We don't have a less threatening nigga store . . . until now!

LTNS: THE LESS THREATENING NIGGA STORE

You don't have to sacrifice your street cred to look great at the LTNS. Here we've taken street fashions and transformed them into the kind of clothes that will put white people at ease!

Before: After:

At the LTNS, we're dedicated to making America *look* great again!

11

DON'T HAVE GANG TATTOOS

White people's heads are always getting filled with nonsense about "gangbangers," so beware: all tattoos, no matter what, will be perceived as "gang tattoos." It's okay for white people to get tattoos of a skull, some weird Celtic symbol, or an arm sleeve that means "Have a great day" in Welsh or Sanskrit, or whatever, but just know that the same tattoo on a black pe will invariably mean "I'm in a gang."

So if you want to have tattoos, mak innocuous as possible. Try to g

Smurfs or that clearly say "Mom." Even then, white people might be prone to seeing your tattoos as threatening.

Tattoos and the Way White People See Them

Tattoos	The Gang Tattoo White People See
tattoo of "Mom" in a heart	tattoo of fist with "Black Power"
tattoo of Calvin and Hobbes, peeing	tattoo of Calvin peeing on a cop
tattoo of a happy face	tattoo of a skull
tattoo of "Simone"	tattoo of "Crips and Bloods"

REMEMBER

RACISM IS TOAST

White people wish racism would just go away so they
ldn't have to deal with it. Here's the problem: We don't
d of racism when we cover shit up. You have to ac-
it, look at it, and deal with it.

It's like when your mother used to burn your toast and you still had to eat it. "Just scrape the black stuff off and it's fine. The rest of it's still good!" No, it ain't. No kid wants to eat that burnt toast.

You can't just scrape off the most obvious racism and say the rest is good toast! Throw that shit out. It's time for a fresh slice.

12

HOW TO DO
YOUR HAIR

What kind of haircuts do white people like? Well, let's look at who they put in charge.

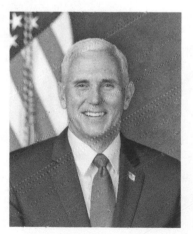

Vice President Mike Pence has perfectly respectable hair.

Treasury secretary Steve Mnuchin has standard-issue middle-aged white guy hair.

Didn't we already do Mike Pence? Oh shit, that's Supreme Court justice Neil Gorsuch. Sorry, all these white guys look the same.

Short hair is the preferred choice for white dudes! With a

part on the side. That's the way white people like their hair. Of course, white people will sometimes overlook a weird haircut:

Sure his hair is terrible, but his views and policies are worse. I don't think that even the most rabid conservative would say they love Trump's haircut; they love him for his demented Archie Bunker attitude.

Steve Bannon looks like a crazed drifter. But he's their crazed drifter.

White hair is no fun. You're just not going to see a lot of variety with white hair. Ever since the Beatles grew their hair out an extra inch, long hair on white dudes has only been for hippies, rock stars, and burn-outs.

The problem with black hair is that it's confusing for white people. That's why people are always asking to touch it. They don't get it. Don't believe me? Up until recently, the Transportation Security Administration was able to take a black woman and search her hair because it seemed "different" to the TSA officers. Malaika Singleton, a black, female neuroscientist, filed suit because her "sister locks" were given hair pat-downs that white passengers were not subjected to. The American Civil Liberties Union was able to get the TSA to change their procedures so they don't waste time with this "hair threat." I mean, the Islamic State is not known for its weaves.

"Different" hair has been subjected to harassment and unfair treatment. Especially for black women. In the army, black women have been told they have to wear their hair in specific hairstyles. The *New York Times* interviewed Captain Danielle N. Roach, who used chemicals to keep her hair straightened so she didn't run afoul of the regulations. These treatments cost her up to eighty dollars every four to eight weeks. Luckily, the army has recently changed this policy to allow for female soldiers to wear "dreadlocks/locks." At schools, girls' natural hair has been deemed a problem and they've been penalized with threats of expulsion, like in the case of Vanessa VanDyke of Florida. Her school told her to cut or straighten her hair, calling it a "distraction." And yet nothing is done about white people and their mullets. It's crazy.

HOW LONG CAN MY HAIR BE?

For black men, the longer the hair is, the scarier it is. But then again, if you're bald, that's scary, too. You have to find the perfect nonthreatening length and style.

Dreadlocks: scary

Braids: very scary

Afro: very, very scary

The half-fro is probably the perfect style. Like James Brown on the NFL Network. Or Ben Carson. It's not really cut short, it's not really cut long. It's in the middle. It makes no statement—perfect for disarming white people.

WHAT CUT SHOULD I GET?

When you go to the barbershop, pick a safe hairstyle. Just ask for the cut you want by name:

Police-Approved Haircuts

You might think that some of these make you look ridiculous; no, you look safe!

SUMMARY

White people like black people to have hair as boring as theirs. If you want to stay safe, play it safe.

- Look at old white guys: that's the hairstyle you want.
- Ben Carson isn't just a genius surgeon and a weirdo—he has great hair.
- If you're having trouble deciding on a white-approved hairstyle, why not try "short"? Or "very short"?

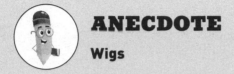

ANECDOTE
Wigs

A little bit ago, Bill O'Reilly was making fun of Representative Maxine Waters because of her wig. Before he got shit-canned from Fox for harassing women, he was on *Fox and Friends*, saying that he "didn't hear a word [Waters] said. I was looking at the James Brown wig."

Bill O'Reilly doesn't understand the importance of wigs! Growing up, every black woman I knew, loved, and respected had a wig. Matter of fact, the wig was an early warning system: if you came home and the wig was home, your momma was home.

But if you came home and the *good* wig was gone, that meant that your momma was going to be gone a long time, she was going to take care of business.

"Where you goin', mama?"

"Don't worry 'bout where I'm going! Just turn the beans off in thirty minutes and watch your brother!"

When she put on that good wig, your momma was either going to church or downtown to talk to white people. "These motherfuckers done cut my gas off!" If she wore the good wig, you knew you could play all day because she was gonna be gone. When she had that wig on, she was going to kick some ass.

So, Bill: You're lucky Maxine Waters didn't have her good wig on. If she did, she might be coming for you.

PART 3

HOW TO ACT

Now that we know a bit more about how cops think and we're look-ing less threatening and dressing whiter, let's put all the pieces together. It's all fine and good to look the part, but now we have to *act* the part as well.

In general, you want to stay away from the words "erratic" or "suspicious." Erratic white people are "whimsical." They get sit-coms made about them. Erratic black people get shot.

In this section, we'll find out what kind of music to listen to, how to talk, get a job, and more! Maybe you've been wondering about whether it's okay to say "the N-word" or what to name your kids. Don't worry; I have gathered a lot of great advice from white folks on these very subjects.

Are you ready to pull it all together and learn how to act? Let's get at it!

13

HOW TO BE NICE AND QUIET

"Will you just shut up and let me finish, Simone?"
—Ken Cuccinelli, a Republican politician
to CNN's Symone Sanders during a
discussion about Charlottesville

White people think black people are loud. They like black people to be nice and quiet.

Let's face it: black people *are* loud. And white people are loud. But loud white people don't have a problem. Loud black people get the cops called on them. Loud black people get Michael Dunn shooting them up for playing their music. So let's take some white advice on this and be nice and quiet like they want us to be.

BE LIKE A CHILD

It's just like my mother used to say: Children are supposed to be seen and not heard. And maybe not even seen. Sometimes grown-ups have shit they want to do. They have adult conversations, they have adult stuff to do, and they don't need to have kids around to fuck it up by talking or getting involved.

It's the same for black folks. White people are the grown-ups, they got shit to talk about, stuff to do, and they want black people to be nice and quiet. This goes for pretty much any public place where there might be white people—a restaurant, airport, mall, movie theater, etc. Let's start acting like children, like white people treat us.

STUDY YOUR ANCESTORS

We need to study our lineage. At one point, black people had mastered the art of being invisible to white people. How did they do it without being noticed? Sure, slavery is a dark part of our history; but that doesn't mean it was all bad. Look for the silver lining: black folks sure got good at being nice and quiet.

True, it was under duress; but in the nice-and-quiet department, we did a great job. Without the beatings, the forced labor, the ripping apart of families and the lynchings, can we still be nice and quiet like white people want?

PRETEND YOU DON'T EXIST

Pretend you don't exist, like the government does. They don't count us in the correct numbers in the census or voting rolls, they don't fund housing subsidies, after-school programs for black youth, SNAP—so in a way you are just doing what the government wants. The Revolutionary War was fought over taxation without representation, so stop representing.

When I was in school, I never wanted to be called on. I sat in the back of the class and I could turn myself invisible. Not because I had some kind of superpower—I just found a way to be out of the teacher's eyesight, just out of her line of sight. She'd turn one way and I'd shift and duck the other. She turned the other way and I'd slouch and hide. But the main thing was mental; I didn't want to be seen. There's a way to not be seen if you don't want to be.

What good has ever come from being noticed by white people? So, start wanting to not be seen. Turn invisible.

SUMMARY

Be nice and quiet, just like white people want. They like us to be seen and not heard, or at least not heard if seen.

REMEMBER

It can be hard to be quiet. You have to want it, like when you were in school hoping to not get called on.

- Be quiet, but not sneaky quiet like you're planning something. If you're too deep in thought, it might look like you're plotting a revolt.
- Or think of yourself as a child trying to avoid getting yelled at by a belligerent parent with a hair-trigger and a history of violence (like white people).
- Think back to Harriet Tubman and others who mastered the art of being invisible on the Underground Railroad. Black folks of that generation had a motivation: they didn't want to get beaten or killed. Times haven't changed much.

14

WHAT KIND OF MUSIC SHOULD YOU LISTEN TO?

"Hip-hop is the worst role model. It's the worst example. It's the most negative possible message, and what's the point of it?"

—Geraldo Rivera

Music is such an individual decision. Does it even make sense to say that there is a right music to listen to? Yes, yes, it does. What kind of music do white people like? That's the right music to listen to. White people enjoy:

- Dave Matthews Band
- U2
- Journey
- That "I'm Proud to Be an American" song

Honestly, all that shit sounds the same to me, though every black person can sing "I wanna know what love is . . . ," even if they're not sure if it's Foreigner or Journey.

The point is, you have to play not-scary sounding music. Like Conway Twitty—the name just sounds safe. And even though Ted Nugent *is* scary, he doesn't sound scary.

Be careful of music that sounds scary. Like T-Pain: that sounds like it hurts. Fetty Wap—who's whapping Fetty? Violent! Wiz Khalifa? "Khalifa" sounds like an ISIS commander, and "Wiz"? Well, white people remember when Diana Ross and Michael Jackson ruined *The Wizard of Oz*—they were not off to see the Wiz. The flip side is, you should feel free to play white bands that truly sound crazy as hell. Yes, somehow the Sex Pistols, Buzzcocks, Black Sabbath, Marilyn Manson, the Beastie Boys, Slayer, Megadeath, Anthrax, and the Grateful Dead are all perfectly fine. I didn't create the rules, I'm just explaining them!

Sure there's good music you can play for yourself, when you know no one is around. But it's smart to have some songs queued up for you to play just for when you're pulled over. Cops know if they hear some types of music nothing can go wrong. A preset classical station is a good idea. Or country music. No one ever gets shot listening to coun . . . scratch that.

Why not put together a "don't shoot" playlist? Like songs by the Police.

"Is that the Police?"

"It is, Officer."

"That's my favorite band. Though I don't like Sting much."

"Me, neither."

"Have a good day, you're free to go."

But stay vigilant! In your rush to change artists, you must be careful not to confuse "safe" and "dangerous" music. Here's a quick list of commonly confused acts:

Safe	Dangerous!
Young, Neil	Young Thug
"roots music"	The Roots
Spice Girls	Salt-N-Pepa
Vanilla Ice	Ice Cube
Alabama	Flo Rida
Timberlake, Justin	Timbaland

LISTEN TO IT QUIETLY

You want to make sure your music is quiet. The easiest thing is to buy some earbuds. That way the music's not so loud that anybody else can hear it. Of course, you can't hear the police telling you to freeze or drop it . . . so scratch that.

Even if it isn't the cops, white people think they can just go ahead and shoot black people for playing their music too loudly. Remember Jordan Davis? Michael Dunn, a hotheaded middle-aged white dude shot up a bunch of black teenagers because they didn't want to turn their music down in a gas station parking lot. So the dude shot and killed Jordan Davis and then went back to his hotel room with his girlfriend. He tried to say he was threatened, but he had shot at them as they were driving away. Granted, this was in Florida, where apparently you can shoot anyone if you want to "stand your ground." But, hey—until the law gets fixed, is it worth it to listen to Lil Reese so loud? Lil Reese is a lot of risk.

SUMMARY
Musical tastes vary, but white people don't want to hear music that scares them.

- Anything with Ringo in it is safe. Stay away from scary music like Young Thug.
- The harder your music is to hear, the more white people will like it.

DLIALOGUE
Leave Politics Out of Sports

"The issue of kneeling has nothing to do with race. It is about respect for our Country, Flag, and National Anthem. NFL must respect this!"

"If a player wants the privilege of making millions of dollars in the NFL, or other leagues, he or she should not be allowed to disrespect our Great American Flag (or Country) and should stand for the National Anthem. If not, YOU'RE FIRED. Find something else to do!"

—Two of Donald Trump's many tweets about players kneeling during the National Anthem

The most hated black man in America, now that Barack is out of office, must be Colin Kaepernick. Trump and other white supremacists have been driven crazy over the Kaepernick-inspired protests of police brutality, trying to paint them as unpatriotic.

Unfortunately, a lot of white people who may even dislike Trump find themselves agreeing with him on this issue. They are mad that Kaepernick and other NFL players keep injecting race and politics into sports. For them, football is about fun, not politics. And yet these highly paid NFL players won't stand during the National Anthem. They say incendiary things about police violence. C'mon! Football isn't about violence!

White people just want football players to shut the fuck up and do their job. So are they right? Are they injecting politics and race where it doesn't belong?

Politics Is for the NFL, Not the NFL Players

The NFL players work for the NFL. The National Football League. Does it say National Political League? No. I don't know how players got the idea that they could be political. The NFL only gets political when it promotes people joining the army. When the Department of Defense spends $5.4 million in contracts with the NFL between 2013 and 2015, I guess I'd call that political. Football has already been political. Think about it: how many times have you heard "The Few, the Proud, the Marines" during a game?

But look, sometimes white people forget about stuff, as is their privilege. Maybe it's an honest mistake. I'm not going to be unfair about it and tell white people who hired a reality star to be president that they don't have the right to tell black people to not get political. I'd never do that. Let's be fair.

I mean, here's the thing: motherfuckers that sell beer and alcohol for a living like the NFL, are they in a moral position where they can judge what's right? More people die from alcohol-related injuries than almost any other preventable cause. They let a football player who killed dogs play. You let a motherfucker that got away with murder play, but you draw the line at somebody making a political stance? Do I even need to get in to the concussion and CTE problem?

But let's be fair: maybe white people forgot that ESPN hired Rush Limbaugh to do commentary for the *Sunday NFL Countdown.* Rush Limbaugh wasn't hired to do anything but talk about football. It wasn't a political move at all! Rush was probably hired for his football expertise. So it was way out of bounds when he argued that Donovan McNabb was overrated, by bringing up race: "Sorry to say this, I don't think he's been that good from the get-go. I think what we've had here is a little social concern in the NFL. The media has been very desirous that a black quarterback do well. There is a little hope invested in McNabb, and he got a lot of credit for the performance of this team that he didn't deserve. The defense carried this team."

So maybe the same people who are mad at Colin Kaepernick for injecting politics into football forgot that Rush basically said that if McNabb was white, he would just be an ordinary quarterback. They must have forgotten about that. Kaepernick is ostracized from the league because he wanted to draw people's attention to injustice. The same league that hired Rush Limbaugh, who made political statements all the time as a commentator, to talk about the black people whom he denigrates all the time on his radio show. He once told a caller, "Look, let me put it to you this way: the NFL all too often looks like a game between the Bloods and the Crips without any weapons. There, I said it." You can't put a racist like Rush around that many niggas and think that he ain't gonna say something that lets you know how he thinks.

And Hank Williams Jr. is back on *Monday Night Football* after comparing Obama to Hitler. Hank Williams is a racist, but I gotta admit: that is the best football theme music I've ever heard. Nothing says "Are you ready for football?" more than people that hate niggas. But that song is so good that even black people are like, "Hey, bring that nigga back here. Come on now."

But I digress. I'm just saying that maybe when the NFL criticizes Kaepernick as too political, they should remember who brought politics into the sport in the first place.

Leave It on the Field

And what about race? Mike Ditka just said that there's been "no oppression of black people in one hundred years." Jim

Crow just ended. I was born in 1964 and I'm the first one of my mother's children that was born with the full rights of an American citizen. No oppression of black people? White people like Ditka only see what they want to. They make up their own reality. The reason they can't see racism or oppression is that they never look behind them. If they're not certain where oppression is, they're looking in the wrong places. Look behind you.

They think that racism and oppression are irrelevant if you're paid enough. They're all saying, "Why are these football players protesting? They're all rich."

Here's the thing with that: What's that common bit of sports advice? "Leave it on the field." Well, we can't Because the very attributes that people applaud on the field—speed, size, agility—are the same things that get you killed off of it. "He's built like a bull." Walk fifty feet off that field and that shit is not an attribute. The same shit they hire you for in the NFL is the shit that gets you killed out of it.

Recently the Seattle Seahawks' Michael Bennett was in Vegas when the cops ran up to him, jammed him up, and pulled guns on him. They yelled, "Don't move! Motherfucker, I'll blow your head off!" And he didn't do anything except be who he is: a big, black dude. He found out that you can never score so many touchdowns, or tackle so many runners, or kick so many field goals or blitz so many quarterbacks that you ain't a threat anymore. The very things he's cheered for on Sunday are the very things that could get him killed on Monday. Being a big, black fast dude is great on the field. Off the field, it might get you shot.

So white people want to us to leave sports on the field, but leave race off it. How? This time Michael Bennett didn't get shot, but like he said, cops pulled guns on him "for doing nothing more than simply being a black man in the wrong place at the wrong time." You know what the wrong place at the wrong time is? Being black anywhere at any time.

If you put *big, strong, fast, agile, fearsome, high pain tolerance* on a draft board, you would go high on the draft. You put that on a police report, a grand jury is gonna indict him. It's almost like for football players: being big and strong is not an attribute—because big, strong niggas get shot first. So, after the game is over, they say chuck all that size, speed, and ferocity, and they should fucking turn into Kevin Hart.

For white people, the game of football is a distraction from their everyday life. That's fine. But even though it's a game to a lot of people, it's a game played by black men. On the field, there are other people trying to hurt them all the time. Off the field there are people trying to hurt them. There's no break for them. One is a game, and one is a game of life.

So race is always going to be a part of football for black people, whether Mike Ditka or Jerry Jones wishes it weren't true. Hell, you'd think the NFL owners would hate police shootings because they're shooting the crop! One man's suspected terrorist is another man's first-round draft pick.

If You're a Big Black Guy, Don't Be

Police didn't just jam up Michael Bennett because they're racists. That idea is so upsetting to white people. They think innocent people don't get slammed to the ground and get guns pulled on them. Police jammed Michael Bennett up because he matched the description of a shooting suspect.

It seems like that happens a lot. We have another case of a big black dude matching the description. Who wouldn't be afraid of a big black dude? That's the subtext, that's the justification for the cops treating him and many other innocent black people the way they do: he's a big black guy so he must be dangerous. He must have done something.

So what's the solution? Get small.

If you're big, look smaller. In the animal kingdom, if you are confronted with a superior hunter, an apex predator, your goal is to be so threatening that the animal doesn't want to take a chance attacking you. If it's a bear or a mountain lion, they always say, "Look bigger, try to be intimidating."

A cop is the ultimate apex predator, and everything that works in nature; throw it all out. In nature: don't show fear, be intimidating. Here: no, show fear, don't be intimidating. In nature, look them in the eye; here don't look them in the eye. Don't get big, get small. You can't get small enough for the police.

At Least He Didn't Get Shot

Well, at least he didn't get shot. That's good, right? I mean, here the police were investigating a shooting and slammed an innocent man to the ground and put a gun in his face, but at least they didn't shoot and kill him. They were just doing their jobs! That's society's attitude about it. Nobody got killed and you've gotta admit: Michael Bennett is a big scary black dude at a club in Vegas after a boxing fight. That's dodgy as hell.

Let's do a thought experiment: Imagine if Tom Brady got thrown to the ground in Boston, a gun put to his head. In Boston? They would tear that fucking city down. If you ever want to see if the reaction to violence against a black man is muted, just do a little substitution. Tom Brady for Michael Bennett. There you go. It's like asking "What if Obama did what Trump did?" There'd be rioting in the streets. The answer is so clear: it's only acceptable because of the color of his skin.

Okay, but take a different athlete: James Blake, a top-ranked former tennis player in town for the US Open in 2015. He's six one, but not football player big. He's a tennis player (a *tennis* player!), hanging outside his nice hotel in midtown Manhattan in the middle of the day, and a bunch of undercover cops roll up and question him. Before he knows it, cops are slamming him to the ground and cuffing him just like they did to Bennett.

I mean nothing can be safer than the US Open, right? That's probably the safest major sports event in America. There's not that many black people there—usually just the Williams sisters—so there's nobody to be afraid of. It's not like at the NBA All-Star Game in Vegas. People drinking mint juleps and shit. Why are the cops so beefed up during the US Open? They weren't there for a shooting. They weren't there for a stabbing. They were there for somebody writing bad checks or something.

So do you need to tackle someone for writing bad checks and slam them to the ground? Even if you're not slamming the totally wrong guy to the ground, not even slamming James Blake, why do you need to slam a bad-check-writing suspect to the ground?

Both James Blake and Michael Bennett know that they got lucky, even though they didn't do anything wrong: they didn't get shot.

Bennett, by the way, is still waiting for his apology. Why? Apparently the cops can treat black people like that without showing any contrition. (In fact, the Vegas police officers' union believe *they* are the ones owed an apology!) So remind me again why athletes are supposed to steer clear of politics?

15

STOP MAKING WHITE PEOPLE SAY THE N-WORD

"Popular culture becomes a cesspool, a lot of corporations profit off of it, and then people are surprised that some drunk nineteen-year-old kids repeat what they've been hearing."

—Bill Kristol, defending the fraternity brothers of SAE for chanting "There will never be a nigger SAE" by blaming rap music

Here we have white conservative pundit Bill Kristol grappling with the "N-word." It is very confusing to white people. They know that *they* can't say the N-word. But why do black people get to say it? Some white kids, like the frat boys of SAE, try to say that they learned the N-word from hip-hop. I mean, if white kids listen to hip-hop music by black musicians, isn't it possible that they learned the "N-word" from them? Sure. So . . . in a way, black people are to blame for white people saying "nigger"! Maybe white people wouldn't say it if they didn't hear it so much!

First of all, they can't be serious. "Nigger" has been in the American lexicon since the 1700s. Hip-hop's been around since 1975. What came first: "nigger" or the Sugar Hill Gang? Who came first: Grandmaster Flash or Mark Twain?

White people don't need hip-hop to teach them this word. I was doing a show at Florida State University and they had an interpreter for the deaf doing sign language next to me. I said "nigger" and her hands didn't stop flying around. Every language in the world knows how to say "nigger."

It seems more likely that the frat brothers of SAE learned it in the same way most white people learn it: from being fucking racists. The SAE charter used to explicitly require that brothers be "members of the Caucasian race." So maybe they learned this song full of N-words from their brothers, not some other brothers.

WHO CAN SAY THE N-WORD?

Fucking black people! That's it!

WHO *SHOULD* SAY THE N-WORD?

Nobody. Let's remember, this is a book of advice *from* white people. So even though *you're* allowed to say the N-word, white people would rather you did not. And nowadays, white people have more subtle ways of describing black folks than to say the N-word. If you want to talk white, try some of these on:

- "Thug"
- "Ghetto"
- "Sketchy"
- "Urban"
- "Ethnic"

That way, you can still *mean* nigger, without offending a white person.

SUMMARY

White people find the N-word confusing.

- Nobody learned the N-word from hip-hop, since it's been around since at least the 1700s. But damn that would be a cool idea for a movie: Ghostface goes back in time to teach the N-word to the colonists.
- If you're white, don't say it!

If you're black, use one of white people's "code words" or go ahead and N-word all you want!

LET'S MEET
Bill O'Reilly!

Bill O'Reilly. Where to begin? When you think of the most hypocritical, angry old white guy you can think of, you gotta think of old Bill here. How many years did he spend on Fox News talking shit about black people in every possible way, acting superior, when in fact he was a serial sexual predator?

This dude is mad at everyone but himself. He paid $32 million to settle a sexual harassment suit and then pretended to be the *victim*. As an old white guy, he's in the most protected group that exists, but he said about his enemies, "If they could literally kill me, they would."

And then he said, "You know, am I mad at God? Yeah, I'm mad at him. I wish I had more protection. I wish this stuff didn't happen. I can't explain it to you. Yeah, I'm mad at him."

So, if God is mad at you, what chance do niggers have? Black people didn't even get mad at God for slavery. And I mean, nobody praises God more than black people. Nobody. But even white prayers must be different. They must speak at a different frequency, like a dog whistle or something. "Don't feel protected"? God was doing his job protecting *them* from *you*. That $32 million is protection money.

But look, Bill O'Reilly has always had a skewed perspective, trying to tell black people about race and what's racist or not. Look, if we let white people decide, we'll never get anywhere. We've tried that already.

Bill O'Reilly even tried to defend slavery when Michelle Obama talked about the slaves who built the White House.

She gave the keynote speech at the first night of the Democratic convention in 2016, saying "I wake up every morning in a house that was built by slaves. And I watch my daughters, two beautiful, intelligent black young women, playing with their dogs on the White House lawn. And because of Hillary Clinton, my daughters and all our sons and daughters now take for granted that a woman can be president of the United States. So don't let anyone ever tell you that this country isn't great, that somehow we need to make it great again, because this right now is the greatest country on earth."

Pretty inspiring. Black people built the White House as slaves and now they're in charge. But Bill O'Reilly had to make sure that everyone knew that slavery wasn't *that* bad. On his show *The O'Reilly Factor*, he gave us a history lesson: "Slaves that worked there were well fed and had decent lodgings provided by the government, which stopped hiring ["hiring"?] slave labor in 1802," he said. "However, the feds did not forbid subcontractors from using slave labor. So, Michelle Obama is essentially correct in citing slaves as builders of the White House, but there were others working, as well."

Well fed. Decent lodgings. Room and board, just like college. Maybe they got to throw the Frisbee around the quad in between work assignments! Sign me up!

Bill thinks black people are savages. When he went to Sylvia's in Harlem with Al Sharpton, he "couldn't get over the fact that there was no difference between Sylvia's restaurant and any other restaurant in New York City. I mean, it was exactly the same, even though it's run by blacks, primarily black patronship. There wasn't one person in Sylvia's who was screaming, 'M-Fer, I want more iced tea.'"

I'd say that the latest dismissal from Fox would mean that we won't be seeing much of O'Reilly anymore, but nobody's been given more second chances than this cat.

16

HOW TO NOT COME FROM A SINGLE-PARENT HOUSEHOLD

"Don't abandon your children. Don't get pregnant at fourteen. Don't allow your neighborhoods to deteriorate into free-fire zones. That's what the African American community should have on their T-shirts."

—Bill O'Reilly, prior to losing primary custody of his children after allegedly abusing his ex-wife

White people like Bill O'Reilly are always citing single-parent households as a major problem in the black community. In 2013, the Centers for Disease Control and Prevention presented data indicating that in almost 72 percent of births to black women, the women were unmarried. Statistics like that get white people asking, is there something wrong with black culture? Black children need fathers in their lives! Why don't they marry? White people get unhappily married all the time. Why don't black people?

DON'T WAIT FOR MR. RIGHT

If you're looking to meet a nice black man to marry, the odds are stacked against you. Why? Because you can't marry someone who isn't there. Because black men are killed or put in prison at a higher rate, there are only 83 black men for every 100 black women. In some places it's even higher, like in Ferguson, Missouri, where there are 60 men for every 100 black women. Let's face it, ladies: If you want to marry a black man, you can't be too picky. There are only so many black men who are not in prison or dead.

MARRY A PRISONER!

Almost one in twelve black men between the ages of 25 and 54 are behind bars. That's a lot of eligible bachelors behind doors number one, two, three, and so on. For nonblack men, it's only one in sixty. Strict mandatory minimum sentencing guidelines, "zero tolerance" policies in schools, and heavier policing in communities of color disproportionately affect black men. Consequently, more black men are imprisoned. Then, when they get out of prison, they naturally have trouble finding work, so they may turn to a life of crime, but they have kids. This becomes a vicious cycle. You can't have a nation that incarcerates this many black men and not have this impact on children and marriage rates. So if you don't want to be one of the unmarried black women with a baby, get ready to find a prison pen pal.

IF YOU LIKE IT THEN YOU BETTER PUT A RING ON IT

When Bill O'Reilly criticizes unmarried women giving birth, he's missing something: fewer and fewer black women are marrying their partners. People are living together, but unmarried. So that's one way to have an unwed birth but not be in a single-parent household. And it also turns out that married black women are having fewer babies, so the proportion of births to unwed mothers is higher. Now, maybe Bill thinks that everyone should get married, but should we take marriage advice from a man who was fired from Fox for multiple sexual harassment lawsuits, many of which were settled so as not to endanger his messy custody battle with his ex-wife?

BLACK DADS STEP UP

Despite what Fox News tells you, black fathers are good fathers. The CDC tells us that black fathers are the most involved with their children, compared to any other group of fathers. For fathers living with their children, 70 percent bathed, diapered, or dressed their young children each day compared with 60 percent of white fathers. And 34 percent read to their kids, compared to 30 percent of white fathers. Even that *Fox in Socks* crap, and that shit is annoying.

SUMMARY

White people don't know much about single-parent households, unless they make the mistake of marrying Bill O'Reilly. But if you want to avoid being in one, you'll have to make do with the black men who haven't been killed or put in prison. Don't be too picky. The good news is, it's worth the effort: black men make great fathers.

17

WHAT TO NAME YOUR KIDS

"We are not Africans. Those people are not Africans, they don't know a damned thing about Africa. With names like Shaniqua, Shaligua, Mohammed and all that crap and all of them are in jail."

—Bill Cosby, before his recent troubles

It's so important to make a good first impression. But people sometimes see your name before they see your face, like on a resume or in an email. That's why it's vital that you name your kids correctly. Yes, white people can continue to get away with naming their children "Britney" or "Newt Gingrich" without fucking up their futures, but you're black! Black people can't name their kids just anything.

Stereotypically "black" names cause a lot of problems. A recent study showed that teachers think students with "black" names are troublemakers. When a child named DeShawn or Latoya was described as misbehaving, he or she was judged to be more severe misbehaving than when a child was named Jake or Emily. Latoya always was kind of a troublemaker, though in hindsight Michael had a few too many sleepovers.

And it hurts your job prospects, too; the more "ethnic" or "urban" your name sounds, the more likely your application is to go right in the trash. A 2014 study showed that names like Emily Walsh and Greg Baker got called back for job interviews almost 50 percent more than names like Lakisha Washington and Jamal Jones. Researchers found that having a white-sounding name is worth about eight years of work experience.

Okay, so maybe you want your kid's name to mean something. I get it. My name is Darryl. That means "beloved." My manager's name is Gary. That means "warrior." But Dayquan means "not hiring."

Black names sound dangerous, too. A different study showed that changing the names of a character in a story from Connor to Jamal made participants perceive the character as more aggressive, bigger, and less successful. They perceived white-sounding names as more successful, even a dude named Garrett. If Garrett is more successful than you, you've got a problem.

In their bestselling book, *Freakonomics,* Steven D. Levitt and Stephen J. Dubner had lists of the top "white" and "black" sounding names:

20 "WHITEST" GIRL NAMES

Molly	Emma	Kaitlin
Amy	Abigail	Holly
Claire	Carly	Allison
Emily	Jenna	Kaitlyn
Katie	Heather	Hannah
Madeline	Katherine	Kathryn
Katelyn	Caitlin	

20 "BLACKEST" GIRL NAMES

Imani	Diamond	Jazmine
Ebony	Asia	Jasmin
Shanice	Aliyah	Jazmin
Aaliyah	Jada	Jasmine
Precious	Tierra	Alexus
Nia	Tiara	Raven
Deja	Kiara	

20 "WHITEST" BOY NAMES

Jake	Wyatt	Luke
Connor	Cody	Jack
Tanner	Dustin	Scott

Logan	Jacob	Hunter
Cole	Garrett	Brett
Lucas	Dylan	Colin
Bradley	Maxwell	

20 "BLACKEST" BOY NAMES

DeShawn	Tyrone	Jalen
DeAndre	Willie	Darius
Marquis	Dominique	Xavier
Darnell	Demetrius	Terrance
Terrell	Reginald	Andre
Malik	Jamal	Darryl
Trevon	Maurice	

So what to do? Name your kids something white. I've compiled a helpful list of black names and their white name equivalents. If you want to name your kid DeShawn, for example, why not name him Steve? Go ahead and try it out.

Of course, if you're famous you can do whatever you want. North West? You gotta be famous to name your kid after your frequent-flier miles card. Blue Ivy? That's a supervillain name. But that's what you can do when you're famous. That's why if I have a few more kids, their names will be Resistance, Stand-up, and DL Hughley The Official App.

List of "Black Names" and White Alternatives

Black Name	White Alternative
Darnell	Dustin
Jamal	Jack
Aaliyah	Abigail
Jasmin	Katherine
Darius	Chris Wallace
Jada	Kellyanne Conway
Malik	Reince Priebus
Tiara	Ivanka Trump

BIAS STARTS EARLY AND DEEP

Assuming this book was too late to get you to change your name to Logan, you probably have a black name. So we know that that name will fuck you. What's messed up is that bias starts very early in school and that's true whether you have a black teacher or a white teacher.

There's no discernible difference between the biases that white female teachers have and the biases that black female teachers have. Those biases start to dictate how you're perceived in school. A recent study of implicit bias in teachers showed that teachers expect black boys to be disruptive, so they look for it. A group of teachers were shown four kids playing and to watch for bad behavior. There was a black boy, a black girl, a white girl, and a white boy. The trick was that none of the kids were doing anything wrong. But measurements of the teachers' eye movements showed that all the teachers watched the black boy most often. According to the Department of Education, black children are almost four times more likely to be suspended from preschool. Preschool! How do you get suspended from preschool? Coloring outside the lines? C'mon.

People have this notion that black kids are bad in school and indeed there is a test score gap between white and black students that persists. And why are black kids bad at school? Black kids perform at a higher level than any other ethnicity in parochial schools. But how you are perceived becomes a self-fulfilling prophecy.

So this bias starts out early. How do you fix that? If you want to prevent the school-to-prison pipeline, you need to hire more black male teachers. Studies have shown that having just one black male teacher in third, fourth, or fifth grade can reduce the probability of a black boy dropping out of high school by 39 percent. So there's a big push to get more black male teachers. But where the fuck did we put those black males so that they could become teachers? Oh right, we put them in prison. Our bad.

WISE WORDS

WOODROW WILSON

"Segregation is not a humiliation but a benefit, and
ought to be so regarded by you gentlemen."
—Woodrow Wilson, twenty-eighth president
of the United States, Nobel Peace Prize
winner, and racist

STUFF WHITE PEOPLE SAY

**MAGA Man #2: "But, D.L.: At
least Trump tried to reach out
to the black community. Most
Republicans don't even bother!
They know black people only
vote for Democrats, but at least Trump tried.
You have to give him credit for that!"**

During the 2016 presidential campaign, Trump made his pitch to black America: "What the hell have you got to lose? You're living in poverty, your schools are no good, you have no jobs, fifty-eight percent of your youth is unemployed— what the hell do you have to lose?"

Despite this inspiring message, Trump only received 8 percent of black votes. Eight percent. You could get more than 8 percent of black people to vote for the Confederate flag. But to Trump's point: "What the hell do we have to lose?" What the hell do we have to gain? What has Trump done that would make us think he understands the black community at all?

It's interesting, because even in his first few weeks of office his actions were insulting. He met with Kanye West, Jim Brown, Ray Lewis, and Steve Harvey: a rapper, two football players, and a comedian. It sounds like the beginning of a fucking knock-knock joke, doesn't it? Why did he do that? Because those are the positions he's used to seeing us black folk in.

If Donald Trump cared about black people, he wouldn't have denigrated President Obama with his birtherism. He wouldn't have spent years stoking racist fears by saying this man is "less than" and that he's not one of us, just so Trump, himself, could become president.

He'd rather black people be football players, comedians, and rappers than to see us be president.

Next time, maybe he should bring David Copperfield in to make our problems magically disappear.

Our Racist President

Even after Trump referred to immigrants from Haiti and Africa as coming from "shithole countries," some white people continue to claim he's not racist. How is it that white men can be the experts on racism when not one of them has been called "nigger" before? America has always needed poor brown people to do our physical labor, poor brown people to do our intellectual labor. But Trump wonders why we can't have more people coming from places like Norway?

Why would they come? They live better there. Europeans come to America like you go to the circus to see the fucking animals. That's why. You come to shop, take a picture where Brad Pitt slept, and to see the fucking animals. It's a tour. You're not coming to live here.

People try to excuse Trump's racism by saying that he's just talking about the economic conditions of the countries where immigrants come from. But you can't call a place a "shithole country" when you live in Appalachia. You can't make that argument when you live in a solid block of poverty. You broke to broke people! When we're talking about exceptional America, that ain't you. Broke white people are living on rich white people's reputation.

OUR FIRST AFFIRMATIVE ACTION PRESIDENT

Give Trump a chance? Isn't it funny how the best-qualified person should get the job unless it comes to Trump? It shouldn't be about anything other than qualifications, except with him.

Trump is America's first blatant affirmative action president. He's incompetent, doesn't know the job, has no qualifications, but got hired because of the color of his skin. He's the nigger that everybody thought Barack Obama would be.

- Gaudy and loud
- Incompetent
- Lazy
- Emotional, flies off the handle
- Angry
- Unintelligent—not bright
- Lots of kids by different people
- Cheats on his wife
- Talks a lot of shit

All the shit you ascribe to black people! He does all of that shit. He's America's First Nigga. So, no: I won't be giving Trump a chance.

18

HOW TO GET A JOB

"I think there's been an effort to either make folks mad at folks at the top, or to be mad at folks at the bottom. And I think the effort to suggest that the poor are sponges, leeches, don't want to work, are lazy, are undeserving, got traction. And, look, it's still being propagated. I mean, I have to say that if you watch Fox News on a regular basis, it is a constant menu."

—President Obama

White people say that they built America. But really, white people only supervised. They made the schedules up and gave out the work assignments:

"Hey niggers, you're on cotton."

"Hey chinks, you got railroads."

"Irish, you sober up and dig some tunnels."

And now in America, we have poor brown people to do our physical labor: Mexicans. We have poor brown people to do our intellectual labor: Indians. If you're not willing to work as hard as a Mexican and you're not as smart as an Indian, you're fucked. If you won't pick strawberries and you can't write an app, you're fucked.

But this exploitation of brown people is getting worrisome to white people—these are jobs that they might want if they knew how to do them. They *don't* want to do them, and they don't know *how* to do them, but they *might* someday. That's a big reason white people voted for Trump: they wanted those factory jobs back. Never mind that if the factories come back, it's not going to be Mexicans they've got to worry about: it's robots. Automation replaces more jobs than immigrants. So they would rather try to turn back the clock seventy years to the industrial age than take a night class? They didn't need Trump, they needed Devry.

When white people aren't mad about "illegals," they're busy painting black people as shiftless, welfare-state layabouts who don't know how to get a job. But with a giant border wall on the horizon and Trump cock-blocking brothers from "shithole" countries, America might face a shortage of brown people. It's time to reconsider black people!

THE RIGHT FIT

When white people are considering applicants, when they're talking about people they work with, they always throw around terms like "the right fit" or "being a team player." The right fit usually means someone who's like them, that is, white. He "didn't seem like a team player"? But we play for teams all the time. We're probably some of your favorite players *on* the team.

So black people can be a player on the team, but not a team player. Okay. Even if you wanted to believe that racism wasn't a factor, multiple studies have found anti-black hiring hasn't changed much at all since at least 1989. However, it looks like anti-Latino hiring is up—so welcome aboard. I wonder who could be driving anti-Latino sentiments . . .

The black unemployment rate is consistently higher than the white unemployment rate, black household wealth is lower than white household wealth, median income is lower for blacks . . . it all makes you wonder what could be making this all be true, if not racism. And since white people are the ones hiring most often, we still got a problem.

DLIALOGUE
"Make America Great Again"

MAGA—"Make America Great Again." That is some bull-shit. When was America great? What time period are we trying to bring it back to?

In the history of our experience in America, it's interesting how often white people say shit like "we want our country back." Well, when you had the country to yourselves, you brought niggas in because you didn't want to do the work.

What time do you want to go back to? I mean, white people were not doing great until we came along. That's just true. The original colonists were always dying of some swamp disease or relying on handouts from the Native Americans. You don't like welfare? Well, what do you think the Pilgrims were getting from Squanto? He didn't have food stamps, so he passed out turkeys.

So you white people were struggling. But you couldn't mind your own damn business, could you? No, mother-fuckers, you came and got *us*. We didn't say, "I wonder what's going on in America . . ." We didn't ask, but you insisted we find out. And then when you freed the niggas, you brought over the Chinese. You said, "Who else can we get now?" Once you got your railroads sorted out, you brought the Irish, the Italians, and so on.

You always needed new poor people. But eventually some of those people said, "I don't want that shit. I don't wanna be a nigga anymore." So then they started hating the next bunch off the boat. So if Irish and Italians are white people now, that's just because they found some new niggas: Mexicans and Arabs. When white people say, "Make America Great Again," all they're saying is make sure we got someone to do the work.

The thing about "Make America Great Again" is this: Trump voters want America to be what it used to be. We black and brown folks want it to become what was promised. You look back; we look forward.

Because for us, America was just beginning to get okay when Trump came along. In 2020, I'm printing new hats: "Make America Okay Again."

ANECDOTE
Crayons Are for White People

America is built for white people. Everything revolves around them, so they never have to think of what it's like to be different. When I was a kid and I was in school, they had these crayons: "flesh-colored" crayons. And we never used them. I went to an all-black school in Los Angeles. The only time we used a flesh-colored crayon was to draw the police or the insurance man—and those are some sad fucking drawings.

"What's this a drawing of?"

"It's my mama talking to the insurance man about life insurance and the police are trying to arrest me!"

"Um. Very good, D.L. How about drawing a flower next time?"

So when we wanted to draw our parents or each other, we had to mix a bunch of colors together—orange and black, purple and brown—because everything is geared for white people. Everybody else has to adjust.

Nowadays, "Flesh" colored crayons are relabeled "Peach." And in 1992, Crayola put out a set of "Multicul-tural Crayons" that came in "an assortment of skin hues that give a child a realistic palette for coloring their world. The crayon colors are: black, sepia, peach, apricot, white, tan, mahogany and burnt sienna." Now, I know some "black" people, but I still gotta share crayons with "apricot" people and "burnt sienna" people that I've never seen? That's what I'm saying: everything is built for Peach People.

19

STOP TAKING HANDOUTS

"Right now about sixty percent of the American people get more benefits in dollar value from the federal government than they pay back in taxes. So we're going to a majority of takers versus makers."

—Paul Ryan

Nothing gets white people agitated like the welfare state! Why should our money be given to others who don't need it? Pull yourself up by the bootstraps. That's something I can definitely agree with white people on. Let's start dismantling the welfare state. I just might disagree about where to start.

LET'S START WITH FOOTBALL

Have you ever noticed how the same people who hate welfare, also seem to love football? I wonder if they realize that professional football is really local socialism?

What I mean is, the taxpayers are subsidizing these teams. The city, for instance, often pays for the arena. Since 1997, NFL teams have built twenty new stadiums with $5 billion of taxpayer funds. They get tax breaks on construction, using municipal bonds that were created to fund roads and schools, not sports stadiums. Cities give them property tax breaks, police to patrol the stadiums, and other city services.

And even though the NFL makes around a billion dollars in profits, up until 2015 it was also a nonprofit. When Congress was revising its rules around nonprofits, lobbyists inserted the phrase "professional football leagues" into the IRS code. Even though teams are for-profit, the league itself was treated like it was some kind of charity instead of a corporation. NFL headquarters administered the league and its TV contracts, making insane amounts of money, paying its executives absurd salaries (Roger Goodell was paid $35 million in 2013), but paid no income tax. Sounds like a huge parasite on the system to me.

AND THEN FLOOD INSURANCE

Flood insurance is very interesting. For instance, if you buy a house in the flood zone and you are buying insurance from a carrier, you pay $1,500 a year, but you should be paying like $9,000–$15,000.00 a year. Why the discount? Because you have the government subsidizing flood insurance. And it's running at a $25 billion deficit. *Politico* recently called flood insurance "the government's hidden housing subsidy for the rich." Why? Well, have you ever checked out real estate listings for beachfront property? Not cheap. And by the way, a lot of these houses are vacation homes. The people in the Hamptons, on Martha's Vineyard, or in the Outer Banks who build their houses in areas that they know are risky, what do they get? They get FEMA-backed insurance, right? Which is what? Welfare.

Welfare don't just come in food stamps or a block of cheese. Twenty-five billion dollars? That's a hell of a block of cheese. Fuck that cheese. I want the cheddar!

Of course, just because your shit floods, that doesn't mean they gonna put it back for you even if FEMA's there to help. In New Orleans, they didn't figure out how to replace that shit. In Houston, they did. In New Orleans, the parts of the city that got flooded were poor and black and a lot of them have still not recovered. Houston is more well-to-do. It's the fourth-largest city in the country. And it flooded because they refused to admit that the entire fucking city is a flood zone. Rather than listen to environmentalists, they decided to build Mother Nature a pool. Every other region of the country that receives this increase in inclement weather has adjusted for it. In New Jersey, they build their houses higher. California, they make them earthquake resistant. Texas: "I'mma do what I want, thank you. Because I'm Texas strong." That's nice, but I don't want my hard-earned tax dollars going to headstrong welfare deadbeats like flood insurance recipients!

WHO GETS WELFARE? CORPORATIONS

So when conservatives say that they don't like welfare, they're being selective. Insurance companies get money. Pharmaceutical companies get money. Petroleum companies get money. Agricultural companies get money—they all get money. But don't give a nigger a food stamp.

You want to cut school lunches, but not cut the $13 billion Boeing got from government subsidies? That's how much in state and local subsidies Boeing received over the last fifteen years, according to a 2015 report by Good Jobs First. What about General Motors? Their $3.5 billion is a lot of money that could be in taxpayers' pockets instead.

I don't want my money going to support these drags on society: if we didn't subsidize some of these companies, they'd fail. I mean, take some individual responsibility!

THE SURPRISING FACE OF WELFARE

Poor white people get more food stamps percentage-wise than us, but we're the fucking poster child. In 2014, government assistance and tax credits helped 6.2 million working-class whites out of poverty, more than any other group. About half of the adults without a college degree that these programs help are white.

And food stamps weren't started to help poor black folks. They were started during the Great Depression but became the program they are today because grocery store owners liked the income. Grocery chains still get increased sales during recessions.

Half of all food stamp recipients are children. And most of the households receiving food stamps include children, elderly, or people with disabilities.

So, yes, I agree—there are too many people sucking at America's teat: too many poor whites, old people, and children!

IT'S EXPENSIVE BEING POOR

It costs so much to be poor that nobody can afford to do it. Poor people pay more for all sorts of common household expenses, like groceries. Why? Well, let's take one example: toilet paper. The University of Michigan did a study that showed that poor households are less likely to be able to save money by buying in bulk. They have less money to put up front to buy in bulk and they're less likely to have access to big-box discount stores that have better deals. Because of this, low-income households pay 6 percent extra per sheet. Only in America can you be too poor to wipe your ass!

"You stink."

"I'm broke!"

Poor people pay more for car insurance, regardless of their driving record. In 2016, the Consumer Federation of America found that poor drivers pay an average of $681 more a year than drivers with a higher economic status.

Add in overdraft fees, minimum balance requirements, and predatory lending practices and it's easy to see why being poor can make you broke.

So, we know that being poor costs you. If you're saying "I don't want you wasting my tax dollars and having babies," well, let's talk about it. Let's talk about why football stadiums, rich people, and corporations are getting welfare while we still have 5.3 million people who are poor in America. Let's talk about why the Mississippi Delta region and Appalachia have lower life expectancies than Bangladesh and Vietnam.

REMEMBER

RACISM IS A DANGEROUS OPERATION

America is like a shooting victim with a bullet near its spine on a medical drama. Let's call it *Heartbeat*. The bullet in this instance is racism. So this racist bullet is precariously positioned so that removing it might kill the victim, America. And look: There's a bunch of doctors, both black and white. The black doctors are like: "We gotta get this bullet out or America might die!" And the white doctors say: "Let's just leave it there. Removing it might actually be more dangerous." And meanwhile, America is bleeding out on the table.

And then that shit gets canceled after one season? C'mon now.

20

HOW TO MOVE INTO A WHITE NEIGHBORHOOD

"Welcome"

—welcome mat, but still be careful about it

White people like to live where they want on their terms. First they got agitated by an influx of black people into cities. After blacks moved out of the rural South in the twentieth century, whites practically abandoned cities and hightailed it to the suburbs, gutting urban areas of its tax base. In one of the most extreme cases, Washington, DC, went from 25 percent black in 1920 to 70 percent in 1980. White flight is real: I saw it myself. In my kindergarten class picture there were two or three horrified-looking white kids, but by the time I got to my third-grade yearbook they were all gone, never to be seen again. You remember "See Dick and Jane run?" You would see Dick and Jane, but by the time it was third grade, Dick and Jane had run for real.

And now they want back into the cities—displacing well-established black and Latino communities through "gentrification." Gentrification is where white people who were scared of niggas move in with us.

But what I'm talking about is black people moving into areas they historically never lived in: the suburbs. Black people are moving there for the same reason they moved from the South: for better opportunities for them and their children. But white people aren't used to that yet. A lot of bad things happen when black people move into neighborhoods and white people don't know them. One of the biggest ways that people get shot is that neighbors call the police on a stranger. Don't be a stranger.

You have to introduce yourself to the neighbors and make sure that everybody in the neighborhood knows you, but in a good way. Not because you're playing loud music or because they're scared of you.

THE WELCOME WAGON

Traditionally, when someone new moves into the neighborhood, people bring some kind of housewarming gift, maybe a pie. Well, in this case I wouldn't wait for the welcome wagon.

You might need to hitch the wagon yourself and bring it to them. Sort of a reverse welcome wagon. This is not like reverse racism: it actually does exist. And it could save your life. So try bringing a pie or some fresh-baked cookies around to each one of your new neighbors.

REMEMBER TO NOT FORGET YOUR KEYS

Even if they've done a great job and brought pies around the hood and met your neighbors a bunch of times, don't be surprised if they don't remember you after it turns dark. At night, it's a different story. You don't want to be the black guy who forgot his keys and is standing out in front of his door, fumbling around in the dark. Remember when Henry Louis Gates got arrested on his own porch and had to go have a beer summit with Obama and the shithead who arrested him?

Whatever you do, don't go knocking on your neighbors' doors in the dark. Don't need help. Remember Renisha McBride? She knocked on a guy's door for help and he blew her head off. Or what about Jonathan Ferrell, injured in a car accident, with a concussion, staggering around and the police killed him after he knocked on a woman's door for help.

Always remember to not forget your keys. If you come up to the door and you realize you don't have your keys, just walk away. Come back tomorrow when the neighbors are at work and it's daytime.

A SUREFIRE WAY TO GET WHITE PEOPLE TO REMEMBER YOU

How do you get white people to remember you, then? Maybe get a dog! White people love dogs. And even if they don't remember your name, they'll remember you're the black guy with the dog. You're "Sparky's owner."

But be careful to get the right dog. They'll remember this dude:

With this dog . . .

But in their memory, he'll look like this:

So, not a pit bull. Maybe a Lab?

Better yet, get a small dog. A Bichon Frise. White people love furry dogs with bows in their hair, or dogs with bandanas tied around them. They like that. Bandanas around your dog's neck and bedazzled leashes and shit like that. You want a dog you can accessorize. But not with a spiked collar.

Think of a funny little dog. One that can catch a Frisbee and bring it back. One that can shake hands and roll over. Nice, friendly tricks.

If you want to be extra safe, a rescue dog is the best kind. Then you can tell the story of how you saved your dog's life:

"I just couldn't stand to see an innocent dog put to death like that. #AllDogsMatter." White people love rescue dogs.

And the best kind of rescue dogs are the ones with wheels. If you can score yourself a dog with wheels, they'll never forget you then. You saved his life; now he'll save yours.

"That's my black neighbor with the dog with the wheels; everybody knows him! He's a great guy; nobody wants a dog with wheels, but that guy did!"

SUMMARY

Being the new black guy in a white neighborhood can be dangerous. Make sure people know who you are!

- Bring a daytime pie around.
- If you lose your keys, find a new place to live; just walk away.
- A little dog with no legs can be a lifesaver. Every time those little wheels squeak, a white person smiles.

PART 4

UNDERSTANDING WHITE PEOPLE

You still with me? You haven't been shot? Great. If you've made it this far in the book, I've got you looking and acting whiter than ever before. But let's face it: that's all surface-level stuff. There's still a lot about white people that's hard to understand. Sometimes they say such stupid shit that it's hard to figure out what the fuck they're talking about.

In this section, we'll dive into some of the ways white people think about race when they do. We'll make sure that you're not a reverse racist, that you're not playing the race card, and we'll talk about black people that white people actually like for a change!

If you're ready to try to dig into the white mind, let's get started on understanding white people!

21

WHAT KIND OF BLACK PEOPLE DO WHITE PEOPLE LIKE?

One of the things to understand about white people is that they don't hate all black people. That is an unfortunate stereotype that will make it harder for us to understand them and learn from them. Let's face it: there are *some* black people that they like. It's just that white people will never pick a nigga that black people like. That's why it seems like they don't like any black people. Because the black people they like aren't black people that black people like.

White people got bad taste in black people. It's as if white people say, "I'm white, but if I were a black guy, I'd be that black guy." That's the guy they like. You know, white black guys. Black guys that always make them feel fine about being white, that always agree with them. Someone who reminds them of themselves. They pick Herman Cain. They pick Ben Carson. They pick Clarence Thomas.

Some of the black people that white people like might be more welcome at a Klan rally than a black church. Let's not test that theory, though.

CASE STUDY: CLARENCE THOMAS, A GOOD BLACK GUY

For black people, Thurgood Marshall was the most successful jurist of his time. He'd argued before the Supreme Court successfully so many times, they just said, "You know what? Let's give this nigga a job." Historians still look at his rulings and writings. He was integral to writing opinions. Now that's a black person that black people like.

Thurgood Marshall died in 1993 and white people replaced him with Clarence Thomas. The main thing to know about Clarence Thomas is that he never says a fucking thing. Clarence Thomas has been so silent, if he didn't take pictures with the Supreme Court justices, they would think he was the black janitor there photobombing them. Last year he broke a ten-year silence on the court to ask a few questions. It's crazy. But that's the nigga the white people like: the quiet one.

CASE STUDY: BEN CARSON, A BAD BUT THEN GOOD BLACK GUY

Ben Carson is another. White people love Ben Carson. Trump even named him to his cabinet. Why the fuck do whites like Ben Carson? Ben Carson embodies the pull-yourself-up-by-the-bootstraps ethos that white people fetishize even though they don't have to do that much themselves. He rose from poverty to become the first neurosurgeon to separate conjoined twins. Basically they like him because they can point to him and say, "See, we don't need to help black folks after all. They just need to be more like Ben!"

Not only that, he even overcame being a thug! In 2016, when he was promoting his book *Healing Hands*, I mean running for president, he told the story of hitting his mother with a hammer and trying to stab his friend with a knife, apparently to show that he used to be a bad motherfucker. What? Most black people try to convince people they didn't do something. He tried to convince them that he did: "I almost killed somebody." He was so boring, he was trying to seem like he used to be bad. How can you be a president with a street rep?

Good thing we dodged that bullet, right? It'd be *horrible* to have a weird dope as president. Nor should you be secretary of housing and urban development, which is the job Trump gave him. But I guess Trump needed a black dude for that position, so why not pick a white black dude.

WHY ISN'T OBAMA A BLACK GUY WHITE PEOPLE LIKE?

It's ironic that white people like Ben Carson because of his inspirational story, and yet a good percentage of them can't stand Barack Obama. Let me think . . . I know a black guy who was raised by a single mother, who ascended to Harvard, has a great marriage, bright children, is a brilliant guy who worked his way all the way up to the presidency! Forget about his policies and politics, how come so many white people can't even admit that Obama is every bit an inspiration as Ben Carson. They asked us, "You voted for Barack Obama, but what about this Ben Carson guy?" You can't pick our black people. You can't tell us "Enough about that Obama. What about our guy?" Both grew up poor, both are black men who pulled themselves up. But one is bat-shit crazy. Barack Obama didn't have to try to stab someone to become president.

Well, after Ben Carson didn't pass muster, Republicans said, "Fuck it, we tried offering you a black option, but now we're doubling down on the racist one." Trump's agenda might as well be called "I'm gonna undo everything that nigger Obama did." I've never seen anybody so obsessed with a black man who isn't a Kardashian.

WHITE PEOPLE LIKE BLACK PEOPLE WHO BLACK PEOPLE LIKE AFTER THEY'RE DEAD

It never fails. White people have terrible taste in black people until we get to about age seventy-five. But then they start liking the people we like—that is, after they're old and feeble. Better yet: after they're dead. In other words, they like the people we like after they're no longer a threat.

They started digging Muhammad Ali when he was close to dead. Then he became an icon. They liked Martin Luther King Jr. after he was dead. Now everyone loves him, but at the time he was unpopular with whites, just like Black Lives Matter is today. In 1966, a poll of white adults found that only 36 percent felt that MLK was helping the civil rights cause and half thought he was hurting it. Back then they condemned him. Now they quote him.

Every black person who got a holiday was somebody that scared white people. Nobody will ever remember Ben Carson. History will remember the people who spoke against what was going on. That's who they'll remember. In the meantime, white people will probably continue to pick black people who make them feel comfortable. They'll pick the wrong black dude for their token black Republican presidential candidate. And they'll pick the wrong black dude in the lineup, sure. But don't count on recognition of who is an important black dude during their lifetime. Only dead black dudes get their own stamp.

Note to self: if whites start praising me and giving me honors, I'd better get my affairs in order, because my days are numbered!

22

YOUR BILL OF RIGHTS

Here's the Bill of Rights:

Freedom of Religion, Speech, and Press

Right to bear arms

Don't have to let soldiers shack up in
your house

Prohibits unreasonable searches and seizures

Protection of rights to life, liberty, and property

Right to a speedy trial with impartial jury, etc.
in criminal cases

Right to a trial by jury in civil cases

Excessive bail, fines, and punishments forbidden

Other rights are kept by the people

The powers not delegated to the government are
reserved to the state or the people.

Here's YOUR bill of rights:

This space intentionally left blank

Sorry! White people will tell you that you have the same rights as they do, but what happens when you try to exercise them? That's a different story.

Am I being extreme?

First Amendment: Did Sandra Bland have freedom of speech when she was taken into custody by a cop who didn't like the way she spoke?

Second Amendment: Did Philando Castile have the right to bear arms when he was shot for having a gun?

Third Amendment: Do we have the right to not have the Redcoats take up residence in our homes? Is this what they called gentrification back then? Okay, to be fair, this one is mostly solved. But if there were Redcoats around, you know they'd be fucking with us.

Fourth Amendment: Did hundreds of black people have the right to not be stopped and frisked for no reason in their own communities?

Fifth Amendment: Did the Central Park Five have the right to not self-incriminate when they were forced to confess to a crime they didn't commit?

Sixth Amendment: Do poor black people who rely on systematically underfunded public defenders' offices have a right to a speedy trial?

You get the point, right?

When you're talking to the police, don't say, "I know my rights." Nothing pisses somebody off like somebody knowing their job better than them. People hate that, especially cops. It's better that you pretend like you don't know shit.

Us knowing shit used to get us hung. If they found out you could read or that you knew something, that was enough to get you strung up. And knowing your rights is really the same thing. It doesn't protect you in any way. It doesn't insulate you. It just pisses off the guy who's violating your rights.

Take a white guy and a black guy and put them in the exact same scenario and see what happens when they exercise their rights. Whether a black guy is exercising his Fifth Amendment rights or Second or First Amendment rights, he's still getting an ass whupping. His first, second, third, fifth—it all adds up to 9-1-1.

23

"I'M NOT RACIST, I HAVE BLACK FRIENDS"

Can you be racist if you have black friends?

The question is: does a serial killer kill everybody? There are some people the serial killer doesn't kill. He has some people over for dinner (*not* Jeffrey Dahmer–style), maybe he's got some pals in a book club. He doesn't kill those people. Who's going to pick next week's book?

A serial killer doesn't kill his friends, but that doesn't mean he's any less of a serial killer. And a racist isn't always being racist. Maybe he likes his black friends but crosses the street when he sees a strange black dude walking toward him at night.

Everyone's a little racist, but some people have a higher tolerance for it than others. Just like everybody who voted for Trump isn't a racist—but I think that they all were comfortable with racism.

People are comfortable with racism for a lot of reasons. Because they go to family reunions and there's racist Uncle Ted. He's a great guy, just a little racist, right? They can't see dear Uncle Ted actively doing anything and acting on those feelings. *Come on, he's just joking! I'm just laughing to humor him. He's harmless!* Well, guess what, put all those people together and can do some horrible shit. A whole lot of Uncle Teds elected Donald Trump.

America laughed along with Trump every step of the way—right off a cliff. *Come on, it's a show! He doesn't really mean it! Don't worry, he'll become more presidential once he gets in office. Uh, he's an outsider and needs a couple months to get up to speed . . . fuck, maybe he just needs the right team around him? The right dose of meds??* Let's hope we don't hit bottom before 2020.

ANECDOTE
The First Time I Knew I Was Black

When I was a kid, I didn't even know I was black. I was just whatever I was. The first time I really knew I was black was when I was about five or six years old. We were on a field trip to Olvera Street, the oldest street in Los Angeles. Everybody used to go on field trips down there—I guess they didn't know where else to take a bunch of little black or Mexican kids. Seems like a shitty field trip: "Oh, we'll take them to a street where they can see how old the street is. Can't take them to a fucking museum, they'll probably knock over a statue or something. No, let's take them to this old street where they have all these old shops and they can buy some Mexican jumping beans and maracas and shit."

And we had gone there so many times that by the time we got there, I knew all the spots. I wanted to go to this ice cream parlor that I really loved. So my friend and I headed over there. And I said, "Sir, can I have some ice cream?"

And he went, "We don't serve niggers."

"Well then, can I have strawberry?" I asked. I didn't know what the fuck this guy was talking about.

"He doesn't serve blacks," my friend said. "He don't serve us."

"What do you mean?" I said.

"We don't want no black people in here."

"Black people can't have ice cream?" I was incredulous. I was like, *There's a law against black people having ice cream? That's a stupid law.*

So I go home and I'm sulking. My mother asked what was wrong. I said, "This man called me a nigger."

She said, "It's never what somebody calls you. It's what you answer to." And then she said, "You'll never have to be what somebody tells you you are." She gave me a hug. "You feel better?"

"Yeah," I said. "Can I have ice cream now?"

She said, "No, nigga, get out of here."

It's true, I thought. Niggas *can't* have ice cream.

24

HOW TO NOT BE A REVERSE RACIST

White people hate to be called racists. And if you try to reverse racism, be careful: you might accidentally become a "reverse racist." Two wrongs do not make a right. Everybody knows that. So how can you avoid being a reverse racist?

DO YOU HAVE A POWER STRUCTURE TO BACK UP YOUR RACISM?

Racism is prejudice backed up by a power structure. So here's a test to see if you are being reverse racist:

- Do you have a system of government to back up your racism?
- Do you have other bigoted and prejudiced people to collaborate from the government to impose your view on them?

- Can you make police departments look at you like you're a threat?
- Can you make banks deny loans?
- Can you charge white people more?
- Can you be complicit in building highways through poor white areas?

If you are just bigoted or prejudiced, but can't do any of the above, then you are not engaging in reverse racism. Congrats!

IS REVERSE RACISM JUST MAKING SURE SHIT ISN'T RACIST?

Yep. Even though white people directly benefit from white privilege and controlling the power of the government, the banks, colleges, and so on, for all of American history, they still think that black people get special favors when policies are put in place to address racism. In their minds, dealing with race is racist!

It's like what Trump said at Charlottesville: when there's protestors against racists, they are as bad as the racists. He seemed to not want to risk alienating his white supremacist supporters, but when he eventually chimed in, it was to condemn hate on "many sides." This false equivalency is rampant among conservatives who look for grievances.

People fighting hate are not the same as those promoting it. Was America as bad as Nazi Germany on D-Day? Was Martin Luther King as bad as the segregationists he marched against?

White people like to say "I don't see color." Okay. But they sure see color when a black kid gets admitted into a college they think they should have gotten into, or if a black woman gets a job they think they should have been hired for. Then they speak up. In Texas, a white woman, Abigail Fisher, sued the University of Texas over their decision not to admit her based on her race. The Supreme Court eventually ruled against her, but more challenges will surely come.

In 2016, polling showed that 66 percent of the white working class think that discrimination against white people is as prevalent as discrimination against black people. *As prevalent.* That's crazy. But it speaks to the threat white people feel when programs are put in place to ensure diversity and equal treatment.

MAYBE WE *SHOULD* BE REVERSE RACIST

Look, if white people still think that reverse racism is a thing, despite the evidence, then maybe we should embrace that notion. I mean, if they don't believe us, we might as well have some fun. Let's face it, white people shouldn't:

Own Guns

Why should white people be allowed to own guns when most of the mass murderers in this country are white? According to *Mother Jones*, 54 percent of mass shootings since 1982 were committed by white men. But when *they* commit murder, we don't say "white people are dangerous." We call them the N-word: "normal." After a mass shooting, neighbors always tell the news crew, "He was just a normal guy."

We have to change our definition of normal. The brother of the Vegas shooter said his brother was "normal" but the latter amassed thousands of rounds of ammunition and dozens of assault rifles. Listen, if you collect dozens of assault rifles, you're not normal. And you're not a good guy; you're a bad guy waiting for something to happen. You're waiting for the government to overreach. You're waiting for a race war. You're waiting for somebody to piss you off at work. You don't prep for good.

Run the Government

The only scandal-free administration we've ever had in American history was under a black president. The guy before Obama started a war under false pretenses that left 4,500 Americans dead and killed more than 100,000 Iraqis. Bill Clinton couldn't keep his hands off his interns.

And look at the fucking mess we have now. I'd need another book to catalog the daily (hourly?) stream of embarrassments to flow from the Trump White House. The inescapable fact is, white people can't be trusted with the government.

Dance

White people are bad dancers. That's a stereotype, and I don't know that I'll be back on *Dancing with the Stars* to defend it. Dancing is harder than it looks, so you know what—go ahead and dance, white people.

SUMMARY

White people may be obsessed with reverse racism, but we know that's not a thing.

- If reverse racism is just making sure shit isn't racist, then yes, we are reverse racist.
- White people "don't see color" unless a person of color is taking their job.
- And even if white people aren't so good at dancing, they can have that. My dancing days are over. It was a shock to see that white people have my rhythm, but I obviously got their credit, so we're even.

DLIALOGUE
"Let It Go"

One thing white people hate talking about is slavery. "Slavery was a long time ago!" they say. "Why can't black people let it go? Yes, it was a blight on our country's psyche and it should never have happened. But you remember too much; that was a long time ago. Can't we move on? Can't you let it go?"

So you want me to let slavery go, but you have Confederate statues in the middle of town rubbing everyone's face in it. It's simple to me. If you want us to forget, let us. Let us. How can we forget about slavery and have thousands of statues up to the Confederacy? It can't be both America's original sin and something to honor with statues. We'll let it go if you will.

White People Won't Let It Go

The events in Charlottesville typify the differences in the way white and black folks see the world. Trump went out of his way to say that among the supporters of this Robert E. Lee statue there were some "fine folks." You'd have to look pretty hard to find those "fine folks" among the full-on Sieg Heil Nazis and in-bred white supremacists. But there are a lot of white people who don't see themselves as white supremacists but still want these statues to stay up. We have to respect history, they say.

History, huh? Let me try to remember who won the war? Oh right: the North. Hundreds of thousands of Union soldiers—whites and blacks—died trying defeat the rebels. . . . What do you think they'd say if they saw Robert E. Lee and Stonewall Jackson parading all over the place 150 years later? I imagine they'd turn over in their graves—talk about respecting history! The Confederacy lost, its ideas were rejected, and the only place I should hear about it is in history books and Ken Burns documentaries. People seem to think that "the South will rise again," and if it does, it'll get its ass whooped again. When you lose, you don't get a fucking trophy.

It's like America was in a bad relationship, but went to counseling (Civil War) and worked shit out. But you wanna still keep the mementos of your ex! "I just want a little reminder of the good times." No, don't do that! Throw that fucking sweater out, I don't care how cozy it is.

We'll let go if you will. White people never want to let go of shit. It's not just statues. Schools, bridges, libraries, airports, streets, parks—all the elements of our civic society—they're named after people who fought to enslave us. Black kids go to school right now in several places across this country named after Klan members. If you want us to let it go, stop reminding us of it. In Jacksonville, Florida, they had a high school named after Nathan Bedford Forrest, the first national leader of the Ku Klux Klan (and a Confederate "hero"). Petitions to change the name failed a number of times, but finally they changed it under pressure. You name a school after a dude whose gig was starting the Klan? And you want us to forget?

Confederate statues and monuments were put up after the Civil War and during the Jim Crow era to make sure that niggers knew their place. That shit was put up to remind us, not make us forget. So you want us to forget? Unremind us! We've got Confederate monuments in California! California? And that ain't even got shit to do with us—we're laid-back. How the fuck is Robert E. Lee overseeing an In-N-Out Burger?

And look—if you're not going to take the monuments down, if you're going to keep your schools named after racists, at least take them out of black neighborhoods. Black people shouldn't have to go to a school named after a dude who hated them *and* that's underfunded. You can't have both: A shitty dude and a shitty school? A school named after a loser *and* has no books? That's messed up. Why would I wanna learn from this guy? How are you supposed to learn history in Robert E. Lee High School on Martin Luther King Boulevard? It fucks up everything. If you want to keep that shit, put it in your neighborhood.

I Blame Google

America could move on if it wasn't for Google. If we couldn't find out you were bullshitting us, it would be all right. But if you tell me something, I google it to see if it's true, and then I get the information that it's not. So much of the celebrated American shit is based on lies. "Columbus discovered America." It'd been discovered a million times over before he got here. You gotta be a dumb teacher to pretend that's the truth. Nobody teaching that believes it. So why does it get taught? Tradition? Hmm, "tradition" is starting to feel like a code word for "white supremacy." It feels like a white supremacist curriculum taught by people who are aware they are lying, but are going through the motions. Nobody believes Christopher Columbus discovered America, but we celebrate. Nobody believes that Thanksgiving was a happy party for Indians and their visiting Pilgrim friends, but we celebrate. And we teach it. All this shit is to remind us that white people are in charge.

I know some of you white folks are feeling defensive now. You're saying "I didn't do it! It was a long time ago. It's not *my* fault."

I'm not saying it's anybody's fault, but I'm pointing out that in order for us to heal, we can't just "let it go." You have to take a look at everything you think is normal, that I know isn't. Shit that's just "history" and tradition to you, often means I'm being denigrated. Defending the name "Redskins" when you know how deplorable it is? You want us to let things go, then you let go first. All this stuff you hold dear is to keep niggers in their place. Whether it's on the plantation or on Martin Luther King Boulevard, it's always existed. You've always wanted us to stay where we belong and stay out of where we don't.

You want to keep statues up because of history and tradition. Tradition is important. At your wedding, you say your vows and have a first dance as a couple. Traditionally, you get silver on your twenty-fifth wedding anniversary. That's nice. And you know I better get a birthday cake and presents on my birthday. I'm a fan of tradition. But maybe not all traditions, maybe not all history is worth honoring.

Put it this way: If somebody sold *your* kids, where would you want to put that statue? Where should it go?

Everybody's mad at Colin Kaepernick and other NFL players because they're protesting police brutality by not standing during the National Anthem. Trump wants to make it about respecting our flag and about patriotism. But let's not forget the history of "The Star-Spangled

Banner." "The Star-Spangled Banner" was a poem that Francis Scott Key, an anti-abolitionist, wrote. Only later did it become our anthem—but we only sing the first verse because the third verse isn't so nice to black people. Go ahead and google it. I'll wait. Key wrote it during the War of 1812, when the British troops offered freedom to enslaved black Americans if they'd fight on their side, which is just what they did. A group of former slaves fought on the British side, whooped Key's ass, and he wanted to kill them. In the third verse, he says:

> And where is that band who so vauntingly swore,
> That the havoc of war and the battle's confusion
> A home and a Country should leave us no more?
> Their blood has wash'd out their foul footstep's pollution.
> No refuge could save the hireling and slave
> From the terror of flight or the gloom of the grave,
> And the star-spangled banner in triumph doth wave
> O'er the land of the free and the home of the brave.

Key was celebrating the death of black Americans. Now why the fuck would black Americans defend their own slavery against the British? Morgan State University political science professor Jason Johnson recently wrote on "The Root of our National Anthem," "It is one of the most

racist, pro-slavery, anti-black songs in the American lexicon. . . . 'The Star-Spangled Banner' is as much a patriotic
song as it is a diss track to black people who had the au-
dacity to fight for their freedom." And why do we criticize
Colin Kaepernick for not standing up during this song today? If we're going to do the National Anthem, let's do the
whole thing. Let's not whitewash it. We can't just cut out
the shit that don't work for you. Francis Scott Key would
be shocked if he saw niggers playing football. Most white
people don't know that history. My daddy did. He'd never
let us stand for it. I'd say, "But everybody's gonna laugh at
me." But still, he'd say you sit down and you pray but don't
put your hand over your heart and stand up. He knew it.
Kaepernick knows it. Just 'cause white people are igno-
rant of their history don't mean it's not there. We'll let it
go, if you will.

Racist Shit Is Hiding All Over the Place

But hey—what's more American than "The Star-Spangled
Banner"? Maybe getting a wonderful summer ice cream
from the ice cream truck. That's nice. Oh shit, am I gonna
ruin ice cream? No! It's just that that that ice cream truck
song used to be called "Nigger Love a Watermelon Ha!
Ha! Ha!" Go ahead and google it. Ice cream parlors played
minstrel songs of the day and when they started driving

ice cream trucks around, they kept the racist soundtrack. Know your history. Clearly the instrumental version drums up sales better these days, because no little black kids are gonna come running for the truck if it is playing the lyrics:

> Nigger love a watermelon ha ha, ha ha!
> Nigger love a watermelon ha ha, ha ha!
> For here, they're made with a half a pound of coal
> There's nothing like a watermelon for a hungry coon

You know what, make it a vanilla.

And it goes without saying that songs like "Oh! Susanna," "Jimmy Crack Corn," and "Dixie" were all popular black-face minstrel songs. Suffice it to say there's no good songs from the 1800s for black people.

And the word "picnic": this is a word that originally derived from gatherings held to lynch blacks: "Pick a Nigger." White people would pick a black person to hang and then gather to watch. The origin of this word is in some dispute—even my cowriter, a nice white guy named Doug, brought up that others have traced the origins of "picnic" to a French word "pique-nique" for a gathering where people bring food. Yeah, I wrote a book with a dude named Doug. I can't believe it, either. That's not the point. What we're trying to get to is this: even Google has its limits.

Take the word "nigger": People tell you it's a river in Niger. Or that it's just Spanish for "black." People will justify the word by wrapping it up in all sorts of history and modifications and disputed origins. They'll say, "Well, it has many derivations."

White people have constructed the way we talk about things for so long, if there's a dispute I say that the tie goes to the runner. "Picnic" might be French, or it might be because people ate some chow while they strung someone up—but tie goes to the runner. In this case, the nigga writing the book.

Look: white people are always trying to gloss over history. A few months ago NBC News had a report that said that they had found Thomas Jefferson's mistress Sally Hemings's apartment at Monticello. "Mistress," huh? She wasn't his mistress. She was his slave that he fucked. That wasn't an apartment; that was dressed-up slave quarters. See? People are always trying to blunt the force of how racist we've been in this country. Thomas Jefferson fucked a black woman, impregnated her, and owned her kids. When your daddy won't free your son, that's messed up. And this guy's on our money—two-dollar bills and nickels.

And everyone got mad about Kaepernick tweeting an image of a police badge and a slave catcher's badge with the caption "You Can't Ignore Your History—Always Remember Who They Are." People can get mad, but he was telling the truth: throughout the South, that's exactly how police departments started. Police in the South were in charge of maintaining the economic order, especially retaining the "property" of slave owners. After the Civil War, the cops were back in action making sure that blacks were staying in their place. That's the direct lineage of the police. That star is no accident; it's not a mistake. It's a reminder.

So white people think we inject race into everything, but somehow they don't seem to realize they've built their whole world around racial superiority, from the bottom up. It's kind of like the air they breathe—they don't notice. They just forgot. Nobody changed anything, they just forgot where they put their Francis Scott Keys.

25

HOW TO NOT PLAY THE RACE CARD

> "Every two to four years, the left, the Democrats, the media, divide Americans by playing the race card every single election."
>
> **—Sean Hannity, August 24, 2017**

Black folks might not have much power, but they do hold one card in their deck that white people hate—the race card. Whenever race comes up in a conversation, black people get accused of "playing the race card."

The race card feels like a wild card to white people that makes any conversation perilous. This magical card makes it an unfair fight: it injects race into a conversation about policing or history or education. "I was just talking about how being a police officer is hard work," they cry. "And you had to play the race card!" Unfortunately, the race card never trumps your gun.

White people don't want to believe race is a factor in a shooting even when it clearly is. They want to believe that race was the furthest thing from an officer's mind. At the same time, they'll defend the officer by saying he was scared because he was in a "rough neighborhood." Huh. If you're afraid of the so-called rough neighborhood, you know who lives there. It doesn't make sense to say that race was the furthest thing from the officer's mind.

So that's what white people think about the race card. We have it and we both know why we have it. We know that race is a factor in many, many things that white people would rather not acknowledge. But they think that black people jump to conclusions, decide things are about race before that's a reasonable conclusion. If we want to understand white people, let's drop the race card and practice not playing it.

DON'T SEE COLOR, JUST LIKE WHITE PEOPLE

White people say: "I don't see color." And that's true, in a way: they don't *want* to see color in lots of things where color is clearly a problem. White people search for almost any other explanation for something. If race wasn't a factor, what was? Let's drop the race card and walk in some white shoes for a minute.

TOPIC: A police officer shot and killed Michael Brown. Why?

"RACE CARD": Because he was black and the cop was clearly racist based on his testimony in court, when he used clearly racist imagery. Plus the entire power structure of Ferguson was set up to punish black people for minor offenses, fine them, put them in prison, and subjugate them.

WHITE PEOPLE: No! Come on, now. The police officer killed Michael Brown because he was a dangerous criminal who tried to grab the officer's gun. Officer Darren Wilson was scared, not because Michael Brown was black, but because he was big! Michael Brown was six feet four inches tall. Very scary and intimidating to a six-four Wilson.

TOPIC: Republicans push to restrict voting with voter ID laws and less early voting in heavily Democratic districts. Why?

"RACE CARD": Because they are trying to suppress a large black voting base that votes heavily Democratic. Strict voter ID laws are meant to weed out black voters just like old Jim Crow voter laws did. It's racism, plain and simple, meant to perpetuate white supremacy.

WHITE PEOPLE: No, no, no. This is about the integrity of the vote! How do we ensure that there is not widespread voter fraud without strict ID laws? Let's make sure that three to five million sneaky illegals do not come in and secretly vote in multiple districts across the United States in a giant conspiracy like Donald Trump alleged. How do we know that this isn't true? I mean, besides the fact that Donald Trump said it. Luckily, Trump appointed Kris Kobach to head up an election integrity commission to ensure that this doesn't happen (again). Kobach was the right man for the job because he led similar efforts in his home state of Kansas, where he uncovered at least six cases of voter fraud. Now, sure most of these were just old white people who fucked up and voted twice, but we'd never know that if we didn't look into it. Sadly for Kobach, in January 2018, Trump abruptly disbanded the commission; from the *New York Times* (throwing just a little shade here): "Mr. Trump did not acknowledge the commission's inability to find evidence of fraud."

TOPIC: Confederate monuments, statues, and flags are still up. Why?

"RACE CARD": They were put up after the Civil War to make sure blacks knew that white people were still in charge—they're pure symbols of white supremacy and there's no fucking way you can even argue that the race card doesn't belong here. The Civil War was LITERALLY ABOUT FUCKING RACE.

WHITE PEOPLE: Sure, sure—there's no denying that the Civil War was about slavery. But it was also about economics and states' rights!

"RACE CARD": Yeah, the states' rights to fucking own people and the economics of getting free fucking labor.

WHITE PEOPLE: Okay, but it's a matter of emphasis. Shouldn't we honor our history? Many brave American— er, Confederate—soldiers lost their lives for a cause—

"RACE CARD": *Slavery*

WHITE PEOPLE:—a cause that meant a lot to them. The South is not all about slavery and don't forget that George Washington and Thomas Jefferson also had slaves. Should we take down statues of them? Where does it stop? And if we don't know where it will stop, let's not start!

THE WHITE RACE CARD

So you like your race card, huh? Well, what if I told you that now white people get a race card, too? Crazy, huh? But a poll of Trump voters after the election found that almost half of them thought that whites faced "a lot of discrimination." In reaction to the Republican Party's discussion of bringing more Hispanics into the party, Mo Brooks, an Alabama representative, put it this way in 2014: "This is a part of the war on whites that's being launched by the Democratic Party."

The white supremacist fringe has taken this a step further, warning that America is facing a "white genocide." Somehow black people, Jews, and other nefarious liberal forces have conspired to get rid of white people. I guess I missed that meeting. But these crazy ideas get a boost from some prominent supporters, like when President Trump retweeted Twitter user "@WhiteGenocideTM."

Old white guys think they're facing more discrimination than black people. And now Trump's attorney general is investigating affirmative action admissions policies that they think discriminate against white people.

Wow—white supremacy, white power, *and* a white race card. Things are looking up for white people!

WHO GETS TO DECIDE WHAT'S RACIST?

- Who here has ever been called "nigger"? Raise your hand.
- Who here has ever been followed by the police just because they were black? Raise your hand.
- Who here has ever been stopped by the police because you were black and with three other black people? Raise your hand.
- Who here has been told, "You're nice, handsome, or smart for a black person"? Raise your hand.
- Who here has been told, "You're so different from the rest of them"? Raise your hand.
- Who here has had anybody ever ask, "Can I touch your hair?" Raise your hand.

So that settles it. If you're not raising your hand, you don't get to decide what's racist. We do.

26

END WHITE-ON-
WHITE CRIME!

It's an alarming statistic: according to the FBI, 83 percent of white murder victims were killed by white people. White violence against other whites is a national problem that is going unaddressed.

Recently there was a spike in the murder rates in 2015 and 2016, after a decline of twenty-five years. In our biggest cities, this increase is even starker: the murder rate increased 20 percent in cities with over 1 million people. Needless to say, the biggest increase was in Chicago, where whites are the majority race.

White leaders have only paid lip service to addressing this violence. White attorney general Jeff Sessions said, "For the sake of all Americans, we must confront and turn back the rising tide of violent crime. And we must do it together." Together? Where is the white response to this majority-white crime?

In 2016 alone, there were 2,854 deaths of whites at the hands of other whites. No other race comes close to killing as many whites as whites do. This is 280 more white-on-white murders than the previous year. At what point do white people start to grapple with a sick violence that seems unique to their culture?

Maybe whites should spend less time trying to reform the police departments who are just trying to stop criminals and spend more time policing their own behavior. I hear lots of white people decrying the use of force in police brutality cases, but I never hear them decrying white-on-white crime.

Only when white people come to terms with the white-on-white crime problem can we finally tackle the even more pernicious problem of male-on-male crime, which grows year after year.

27

HOW TO MAKE
WHITE FOOD

While we're talking about becoming nonthreatening, here's some tips on nonthreatening food. Barbecue tastes good, but smells dangerous. White people are known for food that doesn't offend:

- Potato salad
- Lobster rolls
- Hot dogs
- Mac and cheese
- Chicken pot pie
- Meat loaf

But if you want to be extra careful, avoid allergens like gluten that might offend. Gluten is like the black people of food—food without it doesn't have as much flavor, but white people still like it. Not everyone who eats gluten-free food even has a gluten allergy . . . they just feel more comfortable not eating gluten. It's fine for some people to eat gluten; that's their choice.

Gluten-free Blueberry Muffin Recipe

2 eggs, separate but equal

2 cups gluten-free flour

2 teaspoons baking powder

½ cup softened butter

¾ cup sugar

½ cup milk

2 cups blueberries

¼ cup mix of cinnamon and sugar for topping

1. Preheat oven to 350°F. Grease muffin tin like you're making a donation to the RNC.
2. Mix the dry ingredients like you're integrating a high school.
3. Beat butter and sugar together like you are the cops beating Rodney King. Add the eggs. Keep beating.
4. Add the dry ingredients, mix until thick. Add milk and vanilla extract. Keep mixing.
5. Fold in blueberries.

6. Fill muffin tins with batter. But leave about ⅓ unfilled like a promise to reform the police department. Top with cinnamon/sugar topping.
7. Bake about 25 minutes, until a toothpick inserted comes out clean like a drug test.
8. Allow muffins to cool while the grand jury investigates. I mean, let them cool until they can be removed from the tins without breaking apart. You know, stonewall until you almost forget there are muffins.

Yes, to you this recipe seems silly. But if you give this gluten-free muffin to one of your white neighbors, it's like lost-key insurance. "Oh, I remember you: you're the black dude who just moved in. I thought you were a burglar but then I remembered those delicious muffins you brought me and I thought, that's the one with the dog with wheels!"

PART 5

TIDBITS OF ADVICE FOR WHITE PEOPLE FROM BLACK PEOPLE

I've spent a book putting together a bunch of advice from white people for black people. Hopefully you've found it helpful in understanding what white people think and how to put their white guidelines into your life.

But what about a short section, separate but equal, that gives white people a little advice from black people? Why not? Like I've said, white people are the arbiters of knowing shit. But I bet we have a little bit of advice that white people could use, too. We've spent a book listening to you all. Why not see if black folks have some tidbits of advice for you?

28

IT'S HARD BEING WHITE, BUT TRY TO MAKE DO

We all know it's hard being black. But have you ever thought about how hard it must be to be white? Especially a white, middle-aged man? Everywhere you look (I mean—not everywhere—not on Fox), your opinions and lifestyle choices are being questioned. It used to be that your word was *law*. But now . . . what with multiculturalism, feminism, and so on? It's hard to be a white guy! That's why two out of every three white men voted for Trump.

In 2015, two Princeton economists showed that for the first time in our history, the mortality rates for uneducated, middle-aged white men are rising, while they are dropping for every other ethnic group and demographic. And they're not dying because of some epidemic or because of a war. They're dying from depression and substance abuse issues. They're drinking, they're taking drugs, they're committing suicide. But have you ever noticed that when it's white kids on drugs, it's a crisis; when it's niggas on drugs, it's a crime?

White let them down. "Broke" is killing people. Because if you're poor and white, you're kind of just a nigger with no training.

I've spent the book saving black people's lives. Let me take a moment to save some of my white brothers, too. #WhiteLivesMatter. Here's some advice: don't kill yourself because you're broke. Don't do it. Relax. Do shit like us black people do. Let *us* help *you*.

You know how people say, "What would Jesus do?" Think, What would a nigger do?

You have to think like that. What would black folks do? Not kill themselves! Because we're poor? C'mon now. That's not it. That's ridiculous. "*WWAND?*"

BROKE MONEY TIPS FOR WHITE PEOPLE

So I've got some tips to save your broke ass:

Your Phone: Put your phone in your child's name. You don't have to kill yourself because your credit's bad; just put your phone in your kid's name. He doesn't need good credit for a while. There's no need to be depressed.

Your Bills: If you can't pay your bills, at least lie to them about it. The electric company doesn't want to hear "I can't pay." They want to hear "The check is in the mail." It's just like lying to your girl: "I love you." *I love you, too.* A little white lie keeps the relationship alive.

Your Car: Geico could save you 15 percent on car insurance, but when you're broke you gotta save 100 percent on car insurance. And since you're white, all that happens if you get pulled over without insurance is that you'll get a fine that you won't pay.

Your Job: Jobs are what give you money and benefits. But if you're broke, the benefits we're talking about aren't health and dental, they're free sliced meats from the deli department samples or cut-it-yourself firewood. Hey, it's something.

Your Investments: Maybe you used to play the stock market and miss the opportunity to have your money triple if you hit a hot stock. Well, let me introduce you to *scratch tickets*. Sometimes you can buy a $5 scratch ticket and win enough for two more scratch tickets. Just be careful about making too many "investments."

How to Save Money: Saving money when you're broke is hard. You can clip coupons, only buy things when they're on sale, cut back on things that aren't necessary. Oh, you did all that? Well, look, it's been a while since I've been broke, so why you bothering me with this shit? How come you're spending money on my book when you don't have it? That's the kind of dumb shit that got you in this mess.

So if you're feeling down, don't do anything drastic. Look on the bright side: middle-aged blacks still have a higher mortality rate than whites, although the gap is closing. So shit ain't as bad as we got—yet.

THANKS, WHITE SUPREMACISTS!

I don't like white supremacists, but I gotta give credit where credit is due. When I saw the white supremacists in Charlottesville with those tiki torches, the first thing I thought was, Those are the same torches I use in my backyard to keep bugs away. I had no idea that citronella worked on niggers so well. I had no idea. So now I know how to end my barbecue early: "Oh, hey, nigger, is that citronella? I gotta go. Ernestine, get the kids. This dude's got citronella."

I thank them for that.

29

PAY ATTENTION TO SIGNS

We know that signs are for white people. They're never for us. Whenever they put a sign up, somebody white got hurt right there. "Deer crossing," "Bridge ices before road," "Slippery when wet"—all of them. Something happens to a nigga, they don't bother to put up a sign. So you know if there is a sign, white people watch out.

In 2016, a little boy was pulled into the water by an alligator at Disney World. What the fuck was the kid doing wading around in the water? When black people see a sign that says "No swimming," we figure someone knows what the fuck they are talking about. It was horrible, but that's why they had the sign there. Black people respect warnings. Don't fuck with that stuff. You go to a nigga's house, they still have those tags on their pillows that say "don't remove." A black person's like, "Hey I don't know what that's all about—better leave it on."

There's black people scratching their necks right now because that collar tag is tearing them up, but they don't want to take it off. "Who's Inspector Nine? He must know something. That's not Inspector One. Nine's a high number. You don't get to Nine by fucking around."

And of course, when a black kid gets dragged around by a gorilla, everyone sides with fucking Harambe. White kid: oh, the alligator's bad. Black kid: it's the kid's fault! Harambe got shot for the same reason niggas did: because he was big and strong and people were scared of him. I felt bad for him because, just like my people, he was taken from his homeland, brought to a foreign place, and told to adapt. Then they shot him. He didn't kill that kid. They killed him because they were scared of him, just like us. He basically got shot because company dropped by.

DON'T EAT TOO MUCH SUGAR

Don't do it! Sugar is yummy, but too much is bad for you. Trust me, it's not working out good for us. It's the best advice I ever got from my eight-toed grandmother.

Not specific to being black or white, that's just good advice I thought I'd throw in there.

Oh, also: eat your vegetables.

DON'T GET "WHITE-GIRL WASTED"

Don't do it. Because you'll inevitably reveal that you had sex with a black person or said "nigger." It just goes bad from there.

EPILOGUE

So here we are at the end of the book. We've been through pop-ular white advice on how to not get shot by the police, how to look, how to act, and we've tried to understand white people.

But listen, even if we took all of your advice, some of which I'm sure is well-meaning, well-intended, and well thought out, we've seen instances where it just doesn't work. Nothing is guaranteed.

- You say comply with police orders, we still get shot.
- You say don't break the law, we still get shot.
- You say don't talk back, we still get shot.
- You say be more like white people, dress differently, act differently, and yet the results are not the same as for white people.

So what does work? Go to the bathroom and look in the mirror.

Are you still black? Don't be. The only way to ensure that all these things work the way they're supposed to is to not be black. If you can, avoid it all costs. If you have to do it, whatever you do, don't ever do it on the weekend. If you have to be black, can you just be weekday black?

You know what? Scratch that. We gotta have you fully not black. After sifting through all this white advice, that's really the best advice I have for you: How do you not get shot by the police?

Don't be black.

ACKNOWLEDGMENTS

I'd like to acknowledge all the men and women who were killed by police while I was writing this book! Obviously I want to thank my radio family: David Kantor, Jim and Tracy Robinson, Skip Cheatham, and Jasmine Sanders. Thanks to my literary crew: my man Richard Abate, my editor Peter Hubbard, and my collaborator Doug Moe. Thanks to Leyna Santos; Yvette Shearer; my Comedy Get Down brothers Eddie Griffin, Cedric "The Entertainer," and George Lopez; my road team, Gary Monroe, Lew Oliver, and Derek Robles! My managers Michael Rotenberg and Dave Becky, my agent Nick Nuciforo, my dude Kensation Johnson, my right-hand Sonya Vaughn. Love to my family: my children, Ryan, Kyle and Tyler, and my sexy-ass wife, LaDonna Hughley.